SHARED HOUSES, SHARED LIVES

SHARED HOUSES, SHARED LIVES

The New Extended Families and How They Work

by Eric Raimy

J. P. TARCHER, INC.
Los Angeles
Distributed by St. Martin's Press
New York

Design by John Brogna
Manufactured in the United States of America
Published by J.P. Tarcher, Inc.
9110 Sunset Blvd., Los Angeles, Calif. 90069

Published simultaneously in Canada by Macmillan of Canada
70 Bond St., Toronto, Canada M5B 1X3

10 9 8 7 6 5 4 3 2 1

CONTENTS

PREFACE

Some of the names for it are middle-class communal living, cooperative living, and shared living. These terms describe the lifestyle enjoyed by a growing number of single individuals, couples, and families with children. They have become members of a "new extended family"—"new" because, unlike the traditional extended family, the members are not usually related by blood; "extended family" because, nevertheless, they experience the warmth of living in a familylike community.

Social scientists have recognized the importance of this trend and studied it for several years now. I have drawn freely on their findings in writing this book. But my most valuable sources of information were the members of about fifty communal households. Proceeding at first by trial and error, they have learned how unrelated people can live together successfully. They were enthusiastic about their way of living and eager to share, in interviews, what they have discovered. Thanks to them this book is a practical guide for anyone interested in living communally or already living communally.

I write from personal experience as well, because I have lived in three shared households since 1973. People decide to try communal living for many reasons. My decision was prompted by the breakup of a relationship. She was going to keep our apartment; I needed a place to live. I considered living alone in a studio apartment but thought it would be lonely. So I investigated the large, older houses where I had heard that unrelated people lived together, ate dinner together, and shared the housework.

A group of six people who were looking for a seventh interviewed me and invited me to join them at Ashby House. Like many other shared households, this house takes its name from its street—in this case, Ashby Avenue, which, doubling as a state highway, bisects Berkeley, California. After living there for a year and a half, I became close friends with Paul and Ann, a couple who were also members. Motivated partly by a wish to escape the constant traffic roar generated by Ashby Avenue, the three of us decided to start our own shared household. We bought a house on a quiet, tree-lined street in the Oakland Hills and named it Pooh's Corner after Ann's dog, Pooh Bear. A fourth person, Dana, was recruited to complete our household.

Starting Pooh's Corner was an ambitious step since we knew that Paul, then a graduate student in science, would soon receive his Ph.D. and probably take a research job elsewhere. After little more than a year he did accept a research position in Southern California. Ann was to accompany him, so we sold the house. I looked for another place to live.

I had served on the committee that planned the 1975 Regional Gathering for Urban Communal Families, a conference held in Aptos, California. A committee member knew of a six-person Berkeley household that had a vacancy. Again I was interviewed and accepted — as a member of Napa House, on Napa Avenue. I had been there more than a year when I met Jean. We soon became a couple, and eventually she was accepted as a member of Napa House. At the end of 1978, Jean and I married.

So the five years of personal experience that I have drawn on in writing this book include my life as a single person, as part of an unmarried couple, and as part of a married couple. These years have been brimful of learning and growing, of good times and closeness with others. I'm grateful for this. I hope this book will be useful to others who want to try this lifestyle.

1. A NEW LIFESTYLE

One resident of the elegant old house on two acres of land in a New York suburb is the live-in housekeeper. The other inhabitants are three married couples and their three school-age children. The adults commute to jobs in the city. One husband owns a business forms company, another manages a trade association; one wife is an advertising-copy writer. They could easily afford to buy the house jointly and employ the housekeeper, and they enjoy a more luxurious lifestyle than they did when living separately. But luxury wasn't their goal when they came together in 1972, nor is it the attraction that holds them together now. They wanted to start "an experimental, nontraditional family," and they succeeded. "There's a feeling of security, of knowing that there are people around who know you and understand you," says Henry, who is forty years old. "They allow you to be you, and the more people who do that, the nicer life is."

The nine-bedroom, five-and-one-half-bathroom house is set within an acre of foliage on a hill just above the fashionable Claremont Hotel in Berkeley, California. Ten people live there — six single adults, one couple, and two

1

eleven-year-old girls whose mothers are part of the group. One mother is divorced; the other, widowed. The oldest member is sixty-three. Members' occupations include teacher, published novelist, executive secretary, and retired factory inspector. The common denominator of this group is an outgoing personality. During dinner in the large dining room, there are no lulls in the conversation. "These are people that I belong with," says Ronda, in her early thirties. "They care for me and they don't judge me. I can try new things and nobody will say, 'Oh my, you shouldn't have done that.'"

The three-story red brick house in Denver was once a doctor's residence. Since 1971, it has been home to thirteen people whose occupations include ambulance driver, artist, and medical researcher. The five single people, three unmarried couples, and one married couple consider themselves a community with a family feeling. They have a meditation room for people who want to look inward and a TV room for people who just want to look. There is also a pottery room, darkroom, artist studio, and workshop. But the most important room is the big kitchen where everyone takes turns cooking dinner, where a rotating work wheel parcels out housekeeping assignments, and where people talk late into the night.

The Stanwoods, a Seattle couple who have a two-year-old son, lived in what Les Stanwood calls "an uninspiring little house in an uninspiring neighborhood." Their friends, the Poysers, had two small children and lived in "a cramped apartment in a crowded apartment complex." This was the best they could afford because living separately, the two families were limited financially. But when they decided to live together they were able to rent a six bedroom house with a quiet library, an arts-and-crafts room, and a den. "Once each day one adult takes all three children for two hours," reports Les, a high school English teacher. This gives the other three adults welcome relief from caring for the toddlers. The adults also benefit, he adds, from "good conversation and a fourth for bridge perpetually at hand."

Life in the big city can be lonely if you are single, but the six professionals—most of them single—who share a Brooklyn brownstone enjoy each other's companionship. Their occupations include fashion designer, magazine researcher, teacher, and therapist. Over the years some members of this household have left and been replaced by new people. Other members have been there since its inception in 1971. "I like the people here, and I like the chores being shared by men and women equally," one woman says. "We wanted a place that has a family feel, more a real home than an apartment," adds Flora, the researcher. "Someone cares if you're late, cares about what happens in your life."

The six adults in the three-story frame house on a tree-lined street in Newton Corner, Massachusetts, include a banker, a neuropsychologist, and a computer programmer. One has never married. The others are divorced or widowed. Their five children make up the rest of the household. Phil, the computer programmer, says he joined "so that I could be independent and at the same time get close to people, especially the kids." Both parents and children like this living arrangement. "When I come home at night, I want other grownups to talk to," says Debra, a widowed college teacher. "My son was living in a totally female world," says Mary Ann, a former teacher. "It's healthier for him to have some men in his life." One of the popular activities the entire group participates in is taking the kids on trips to the country or the ballet.

A "FAMILY" BY CHOICE

Independently of one another, the groups described here have made a discovery of great social significance for our era — an era in which people are experiencing a growing sense of isolation. They have discovered that you don't have to be related by blood or marriage to become part of a warm, supportive household that feels like a family or a miniature community. What's more, their discovery is being made over and over again. In the last few years, households like these have sprung up in cities and suburbs all over the United States. This increasingly popular new lifestyle is now available to practically anyone who wants to try it.

These households don't accord with stereotyped notions of what living in a group is like. Members of these groups haven't withdrawn from society — they don't follow a guru or require one another to hold any faith in common. Their goal is simply to live together in a way that is caring and fun.

Although social scientists and journalists have also taken an interest in this growing social phenomenon and have documented it, people remain unaware of this new lifestyle. One reason that we aren't better known is semantic. We can't agree on what to call our households. We use a half-dozen names to describe what we are trying to do, and this makes it harder to see that we are all aiming at roughly the same things and that an important social trend is under way. One name, "extended family," is favored by some groups because it conjures images of the old-fashioned extended families that were prevalent a few generations ago. The core of these big families was a married couple, but under the same roof lived grandparents, aunts and uncles, perhaps an unrelated friend or co-worker, and of course children. Nostalgic accounts stress the warmth that these families generated and deemphasize the squabbles that occurred between family members of different generations. Aware that living with biological relatives can sometimes be difficult, some people who live communally use the term "intentional family" or "intentional community" to describe their households. Their use of the word "intentional" emphasizes the fact that they have deliberately chosen both their lifestyle and the people they want to live with as "relatives."

"Expanded family" and "alternative family" are further variations on the family theme. "Cooperative household" is another popular name, one that stresses the practical advantages of this new lifestyle—reduced living costs, for example. Another term, "collective household," has a socialist ring and is often used by people who view living together as having political as well as personal meaning. "Shared household" is a politically neutral term that has recently gained popularity and is one that I will use interchangeably with the term "commune" throughout the book.

The social scientists have, inevitably, introduced labels of their own. Their terms include "living group," which is straightforward but not sufficiently explanatory, and "multi-adult household," which overlooks the presence of children in many households. But the names they favor most are "urban commune," "communal household," and "middle-class commune." "Middle-class" indicates that the people in a group are not dropouts or cultists; most of them go off to work in the morning, many hold professional jobs, and their houses generally resemble those of middle-income families. But are these households really communes? The social scientists agree that they are. They define a commune as any group of five or more people, most of whom are unrelated by blood or marriage, who choose to live together for any reason beyond mere convenience.

Although sociologically correct, use of the word "commune" may have unpleasant connotations for some people. The "hippie" crash pads and communes of the 1960s received a staggering amount of news coverage—so much coverage that, even today, when some people hear the word commune their first thoughts are of hippies who engage in free love, use psychedelic drugs, and recoil from hard work and achievement. So it is still occasionally necessary to point out that members of middle-class communes aren't hippies.

We haven't made page one as the hippies did, but we are appearing on inside pages, and this has given us a more respectable image. One typical article, in the *Chicago Tribune*, noted, "More and more frequently, professional people in their late 20s and 30s are choosing to live communally, viewing it as a preferable—and quite respectable—alternative." The *Tribune* quoted a liquor-store manager who lives communally: "The stigma of the thing is gone. Communes are coming out of the closet."

A COMMUNAL HISTORY

In or out of the closet, communes are not a recent phenomenon. They have existed in America since colonial times. Because an understanding of communes of the past will help us view contemporary shared households more clearly, this history is worth recalling briefly.

Religious Communes

The first communes were established by religious sects that fled persecution in Europe as early as 1680. Members of one sect, the Society of True Inspiration, arrived in the United States from Germany in 1842, settling first near Buffalo, New York, then founding seven farming villages known as the Amana Colonies, in Iowa. In 1932, the members reorganized to become two separate entities: a church and a business cooperative, both of which survive today. There are currently about fifteen hundred members who, in addition to farming, operate a woolen mill, two meat markets, and other industries.

Another religious settlement, the Oneida Community in Upstate New York, was founded in 1848 by a group of religious believers who were fleeing not from Europe but from Putney, Vermont, where their leader, John Humphrey Noyes, had been accused of adultery. A graduate of Yale Theological Seminary, Noyes was an unorthodox thinker who believed that "the marriage supper of the Lamb is a feast at which every dish is free to every guest." Accordingly, the approximately two hundred people who made up the community were joined in "complex marriage," enabling any mutually willing pair to have sexual intercourse. But sex was not the organizing principle of Oneida. Members considered themselves to be one large family, a sentiment expressed in the Oneida song.

> We have built us a dome
> On our beautiful plantation,
> And we all have one home,
> And one family relation.

At first the plantation barely sustained itself by farming. Then Sewell Newhouse, an inventor of steel traps, joined Oneida and brought prosperity through manufacturing. Traps, traveling bags, silverware, and other articles were produced. Two of the enterprises were headed by women, and equality of the sexes was partially achieved in domestic life as well. Oneida became a thriving and, by most accounts, a happy community until around 1870, when a new generation of communally reared children came of age. Not having grown up in the fervent religious climate of the 1840s, this generation was less committed to the founders' beliefs. The internal rifts that appeared widened increasingly. Finally Noyes himself proposed that complex marriage be abandoned, and it was. Two years later, in 1881, the commune converted itself into a joint-stock company that operates today as a successful silverware manufacturing business.

Socialist Utopias

Religious groups were not the only founders of historical communes. Around 1820, a second wave of communes—these motivated by socialist belief—began to wash over the country. The most famous, Brook Farm, was not a socialist venture initially. It was organized in 1841 at West Roxbury, Massachusetts, by the Reverend George Ripley, a former minister and member of the Transcendental Club of Boston. Brook Farm aimed to unite the thinker and the worker in a society of cultivated persons. Nathaniel Hawthorne and Charles A. Dana were two of the commune's original members, and Ralph Waldo Emerson was a frequent visitor. Brook Farm's weekly magazine, *The Harbinger*, published articles by James Russell Lowell, John Greenleaf Whittier, and Horace Greeley. Many of the seventy to eighty members were teachers who operated a nursery school, primary school, and college preparatory school. There were also farmers and craftsmen. After 1844, Brook Farm adopted some of Charles Fourier's socialist theories, including the notion that communal living could best be accomplished in an immense central building known as a phalanstery. All available funds were put into the construction of such a building. It burned to the ground immediately after completion. Brook Farm never recovered from the blow and disbanded in 1849.

The socialist communes planned to do away with society's unequal distribution of wealth, but their utopian ideals were not grounded on a workable plan of action. "I come to this country to introduce an entire new system of society," announced English industrialist Robert Owen in 1825, the year he founded New Harmony in Indiana. He thought that three years would be sufficient time to create an "enlightened social system which shall gradually unite all interests into one and remove all causes for contest between individuals." About eight hundred men, women, and children answered Owen's call. Handicapped by the absence of any practical blueprint for the new society, plagued by the presence of idlers since no effort was made to screen the participants, and worn down by internal strife, they were quickly disillusioned. New Harmony disbanded in 1827, after only two years.

Counterculture Communes

It wasn't until 1965 that the third wave of American commune founding began, with hippies in a starring role. More than a million people were probably involved, many more than had taken part in earlier communal movements. Sociologist Hugh Gardner estimates that five to ten thousand rural groups and additional thousands of urban communes were formed during this period. The initial impetus came from middle-class youths, twenty to thirty years old, who were in rebellion not only against the war in Vietnam but also against parental and all other forms of authority. They hoped to create a utopian "counterculture" free of the social ills of the traditional culture. But their antiauthoritarian, or anarchist, communes tended to collapse when members found that they could not live and work together in an absence of agreed-upon rules.

As the early counterculture optimism waned, the pendulum began to swing from anarchism to the opposite extreme. Authoritarian communes with charismatic leaders who handed down prescribed spiritual beliefs and rules of conduct began to attract more adherents. It is sometimes assumed that the rural communes that became famous during the nineteen sixties have died out. Gardner estimates, however, that a thousand still exist. Today, rather than seeing themselves as part of a radical political movement, many rural commune members belong to the back-to-the-land movement of people who wish to escape the cities and live in relative self-sufficiency and greater harmony with nature.

Middle-Class Communes

Occasionally I hear of a group of unrelated adults who lacked strong religious or political motives and were living together communally in one city or another back in the nineteen forties or fifties. A few isolated households like these have probably always existed, but middle-class communes did not appear in noticeable numbers until approximately 1970. The first of these households were most likely formed by people who had read about the counterculture groups and believed that they could adapt communal living to their needs. When these early middle-class groups succeeded, they were quickly imitated. The *Wall Street Journal* spotted the trend in 1972 and assigned a reporter to investigate middle-class communes in Minneapolis, Boston, Philadelphia, Washington, D.C., Cambridge, Brooklyn, Cleveland, and Denver. In Minneapolis, the reporter discovered that a tax consultant, a minister, and a college professor were among the eight adults and eleven children inhabiting an elegant mansion built in the 1890s. In Boston, she found a sixty-four-year-old widow who had felt "practically useless" until she joined a four-family household and helped care for its children. Outside Baltimore, she found that a new extended family had purchased a country house with twenty-five rooms, eleven fireplaces, and a "library so large that the bank appraiser called it a ballroom."

Similar groups formed in other cities, although most lived in large houses rather than mansions. By 1974, sociologist Rosabeth Kanter had counted "more than two hundred identifiable communal households" in metropolitan Boston, including at least a dozen in one prestigious suburb, and she had contacted more groups in New Orleans and Los Angeles. Dennis Jaffe, a family therapist who was then a member of Kanter's research team, found more than fifty households in New Haven, Connecticut, and reported that their number was growing steadily. Middle-class communes also became firmly established in the San Francisco Bay area. In the East Bay, across from San Francisco, a business called the Berkeley Connection was started to refer people wanting to join one of these groups to a compatible household. Although Berkeley is a university town, few of those using the service are students. During one typical week, applicants included a physician, a psychologist, and a former Yale dean of women. By 1978, the *San Francisco Chronicle* estimated the total population of communal households in Berkeley alone as close to six thousand.

But what about an official, national figure for the communal population? The U.S. Census Bureau will count communes and their members for the first time in 1980. Bureau officials say they may need several years to process this data, so a national figure won't be available until 1982 or even later.

Yesterday versus today and tomorrow. As I suggested in my overview of historical communes, the more colorful religious, political, and counterculture groups of the past have some similarities to contemporary communal households. The founders of historical communes believed that by living as a cooperative community or family they could create a better life. Members of the contemporary communes share this belief in the success of social innovation. And they value the daily contact with one another that communal living makes possible.

Beyond that, some obvious differences separate historical communes from present-day communal households. People don't join a middle-class commune to find utopian solutions for all the problems of society. Their more modest goal is, as I have said, to create a home that feels like a family or a miniature community.

Middle-class communes are organized differently from historical communes. The anarchist groups had no rules; the authoritarian ones, a great many rules. Middle-class communes strike a balance between these two extremes. We have no leaders and we believe strongly in equality—yet unlike anarchist commune members we understand that living together works only if we are willing to make agreements and to hold house meetings where complaints can be aired and problems worked through. We agree, for example, on who will take the garbage out and on how other housekeeping chores will be accomplished. But we are careful to keep these arrangements flexible and to have only enough of them to make life more pleasant, not unnecessarily complicated.

Members of communal households don't live for an ideology, as members of historical communes sought to do; but we do have an ideology of sorts, based on our belief in equality. Traditional families have a head of the household; we do not. We arrive at our important decisions democratically by consensus. Even today, men are more equal than women in traditional families, especially in their exemption from housekeeping chores. By contrast, in a communal household, cleaning, cooking, and shopping rotate. Men and women do the same work and have an equal voice in decisions. Our "ideology" is more readily apparent in what we do than in what we say.

COMMUNAL LIFE: FULFILLING MANY NEEDS

Although we don't make many ideological statements, we are more talkative on other subjects. Ask why someone lives communally and you will probably get an explanation touching on five or six major points.

One motive is economic. For example: three families or six or seven single people may share a gracious, older house — the kind of house that was built with plenty of space for the much larger families of two or three generations ago. Everyone gets a private bedroom and shares ample living space. But the rent or house payments are split three, six, or seven ways. A single member's share of the housing costs may be as little as a hundred dollars a month or even less in certain cases. Because utility and food costs are shared, they are sharply reduced as well. The two families who rent a house together in Seattle — the Stanwoods and Poysers mentioned at the beginning of this chapter — found that communal living cut their utility and food bills by about 40 percent.

The low cost of communal living allows people with

modest incomes to live in the kind of home that, alas, has grown far too costly to build today — a solid house with carved woodwork, high ceilings, a fireplace, and a stained-glass window, with trees and a backyard, and in a pleasant neighborhood of similar houses. Many people are able to enjoy life in such a house only because they live communally.

People with moderate or high incomes accumulate an impressive cash surplus while living communally. Often they spend it on travel or on a country home (sometimes the group buys one together). But people who are drawn to communal living for the economic advantages alone tend to be disappointed. Communal living seems to work when people have a genuine desire to become involved with one another as people, not just as partners in a plan to acquire possessions or enjoy a more luxurious lifestyle.

Efficiency is another motivation for living communally. People who don't like having to spend several hours a week keeping house find that shared housekeeping requires only a fraction of that time. Most commune members clean their own room plus one common room. Because they take turns cooking and grocery shopping, members of most groups cook one night a week and shop about once a month. When a group has small children, members can take turns baby-sitting. Parents who once had to stay home with their kids now hold a job or attend classes.

Some Americans feel trapped in a high-consumption lifestyle that supports a high rate of industrial production, which in turn causes continued pollution. These people are motivated to live communally because of their concern for the environment. Three families who decide to share a house no longer need three stoves, three blenders, three washers and dryers, three swing sets, or three newspaper subscriptions; one of each will do. Communal households surveyed in Minneapolis had far

fewer appliances per capita than the average family
household. Per capita natural-gas consumption was 40
percent less than that of the average household.

Concern for personal growth is another motivation for
living communally. At work people learn to function as a
polite and efficient team and to avoid more personal
contact with one another, since that might impair their
efficiency. Living communally, people learn to make
personal contact. Almost inevitably, they gain in self-
understanding and in the ability to communicate and to
be assertive.

Some people are motivated to live communally because it can open the door to another kind of personal
growth. These people find their jobs dissatisfying and
yearn to do more fulfilling work. Because of the decrease
in their living costs, commune members find it possible
to give up their nine-to-five jobs and do something more
rewarding. Before I lived communally, I was a newspaper reporter. When I fell asleep in a school board
meeting that I was supposed to be covering, I was forced
to admit to myself that I had grown bored with my job. I
joined a communal household, cutting my living expenses to less than four hundred dollars a month. With
the emotional support of my housemates I got up the
courage to quit my job and begin writing books. Other
commune members abandon traditional careers to support themselves by making crafts, leading growth workshops, or pursuing some other form of self-employment.
Commune members who want to make a more conventional career change are often able to finance a return to
school. Members who have become disillusioned with
careers sometimes take part-time jobs, using the rest of
their time to launch artistic or political projects, or to
follow their creativity in some other direction.

There are many motives for living communally. But
there is one underlying motivation that is the most important reason people join or start communal house
holds. When a sociologist asked members of Boston

households about the satisfaction of communal living, the great majority checked one box on the questionnaire. It read, "companionship, security, and a supportive atmosphere."

Only a generation or two ago "companionship" and "a supportive atmosphere" were more readily available. Many Americans knew their neighbors, took pride in their city or town, and felt personally connected with other people. Today a lot of us move to another city every few years. Less companionship is available in the typical family, which has shrunk to the nuclear couple and perhaps one or two children. Most of us work in impersonal bureaucracies where the atmosphere is hardly supportive. As a result of all these changes, there is a widespread feeling that a vital sense of personal connection with other people is missing from American life.

Communal living is a good way to restore this connection. Couples, it is true, already have one connection — with each other. They are often drawn to communal living because they want to be part of a miniature community, one that may include several couples. Single, divorced, and widowed people have a whole family to gain by living communally. Because so many single people are looking for romantic relationships, it is often hard to establish a nonsexual friendship. Living communally, single men and women find it relatively easy to have supportive friendships with the opposite sex. For couples, single people, young people, and old people, communal living is an excellent path to the sense of family or community that seems to be lacking in so many lives.

Because the social forces that created this lifestyle haven't diminished, it seems safe to predict that the number of people living communally will continue to grow. We remain a people on the move from city to city, and for this and other reasons companionship and personal relationships remain scarce commodities. The women's movement continues to encourage more egalitarian lifestyles, and the environmental movement continues to encourage lifestyles that make wiser use of natural resources.

As the number of people living communally expands, so does the possibility of establishing networks of people who have chosen this lifestyle. People who live communally gather every year at conferences in various cities to exchange information about what works or doesn't work in their households and to set up networks that enable members of different communes to barter goods and services. Out of these conferences have come many lasting friendships and a dream—as yet unrealized— that large numbers of households will be able to establish an ongoing "community of communities." The growth of this community of communities could be the next chapter in the evolution of communal households.

THE DETAILS OF SHARED LIVING

If you have read this far, chances are you are intrigued by communal living and have some questions. The questions that follow will be answered in the rest of this book.

Are All Shared Households Alike?

Shared households come in a variety of types. This is fortunate, because individuals have varied needs. Some communal households are formed by two or more nuclear families, or by a collection of single parents. In these groups childrearing is likely to be an important purpose. But other households have no kids and are built around either a shared interest or a diversity of interests. A cluster community isn't a shared household, but rather an apartment building or a grouping of single-family homes whose residents want to create an extended family feeling. The cluster community is included here because successful clusters achieve the same goals that shared households do. There are households for older people, for women only, and for men only. Some households are an attempt to pool resources and live in luxury. Others are formed by people interested in personal growth. And there are still more types. There may be a shared household near where you live that fits your needs. If not, you can start one.

The different types of households are described in Chapter Two.

How Close Do Members of a Communal Household Get?

Many people like the idea of getting close to others in a communal household but have questions about what this will mean. Some frequently asked questions are: Will people want me to get closer than I want to get? What about privacy—will I lose too much? How do couples fit in, and how does living communally affect a couple's relationship with one another? What kind of relationships do children establish with other commune members? What happens sexually in communal households?

Different levels of closeness prevail in different households. If you are a person who wants to keep some things about yourself private, you can find a commune where other people feel the same way. On the other hand, if you would enjoy living with a group of people who freely share their most personal feelings with one another, that too is available. People tend to worry about privacy before they move into a cooperative living situation and to stop worrying once they are living cooperatively. The biggest complaint involves noise, which can be bother some occasionally, especially if your bedroom adjoins the kitchen.

Usually without great difficulty, couples manage to strike a balance between the amount of time they devote to each other and the time they devote to other members of the group. They usually find that their relationship becomes less dependent and more intimate when they live communally, although communal living will not

save a marriage already in serious trouble. Children who
live communally become less dependent on their parents. They establish their own relationships with other
members of the household.

What happens sexually depends on what people
want. Some groups are composed only of monogamous
couples or of single people whose romantic partners live
elsewhere. However, it is fairly common for two single
members of a household to have an affair. A few groups,
formed by people who are hoping to find a workable
alternative to monogamy, actively encourage non-
monogamous sexual activity.

Questions about closeness and sex are answered in
detail in Chapter Three.

How Do Commune Members Resolve Conflicts?

Conflict is inevitable in the nuclear family. It is just as
inevitable in the new extended family. The solution isn't
to avoid conflict, but to deal with it effectively, and this is
what communes must set out to do. The first step is to
make sure when the group is being formed that expectations are not too divergent. It is particularly important to
find out how close people expect to become and how
many activities they expect to engage in as a group. Once
you are living together, the goal is to resolve conflicts as
they occur. This prevents resentments from building up.
Commune members find that the more assertive they
are, the less conflict they have to deal with. The ability to
take responsibility for your own feelings is also extremely useful in communal living.

Conflict is the subject of Chapter Four. But one means
of dealing with conflict—the house meeting—is so important that I have devoted most of Chapter Five to it.

How Do Commune Members Make Decisions?

There isn't any father figure making decisions in a communal household. Major decisions are almost always
arrived at by consensus in a house meeting. Some
groups hold weekly house meetings, while others call a

meeting when a member requests one. One purpose of the house meeting is to handle communal "business" — to decide how chores will be done or to consider the admission of a new member, for example. The other purpose is emotional. A member who has a complaint needs a chance to air it and be reassured that the others care. This reassurance is provided when members listen to one another in a meeting.

Minor decisions are often made informally. Usually a member who has special expertise in gardening or home repairs, for example, makes decisions in that area without having to consult the others. Members who want to undertake a project can ask each of the others if they have any objection. The project goes ahead if nobody objects. Sometimes members make unilateral decisions, but these decisions often provoke opposition.

I discuss decision making in Chapter Five.

How Do Commune Members Share Household Duties, Food, and Belongings?

In a traditional family, the housewife organizes the household duties and does the work. There isn't any housewife in a commune. Everyone must agree on what chores should be created, and then a method must be found to make sure the chores are actually done. Because people are accustomed to different levels of neatness and cleanliness, agreement on housekeeping questions isn't automatic. Agreement becomes more elusive when men do not fully accept cleaning as men's work, or when members insist that their personal standards of house keeping are the only right ones. Fortunately there are ways to discuss these issues productively, and communes do manage to get housekeeping under control.

Many households have a communal dinner five nights a week, although members who would rather be somewhere else on a particular night aren't required to eat at home. Some groups have a carefully worked-out system for menu planning and grocery shopping, but others do remarkably well without a system. Members with different dietary preferences can coexist quite happily in a commune provided they do not try to force their beliefs about food on one another.

Rather than share all belongings, commune members decide which things they want to reserve for their private use and which things they want to share. Thus, you might decide to put the pots and pans that you bring from your former residence in the kitchen, where everyone can use them, while keeping some delicate crystal glasses in your room where they will remain private and unbroken. In some households, the living-room couch belongs to John, the piano is Elizabeth's, the dining table and chairs are Dave's, and so on. Well-established communes often own the furniture, rugs, and other furnishings as a group, and have a fund to replace these items as they wear out.

In communes that have children, parents retain the principal responsibility for their own kids. Childcare is shared to a degree that varies from household to household. Adults may take turns baby-sitting, driving kids to school, and taking them on excursions, for example. The full benefits of shared childcare are realized only when a group recognizes the fact that adults have different child-rearing styles and manages to accommodate these differences. A group can agree to accept a difference, or it can adopt a "community standard" that everyone feels comfortable with. Sometimes childrearing styles are so different that the adults can't get them to mesh. This is something that parents should take pains to discover in advance, before they decide to live with other people.

The sharing of household duties, food, belongings, and childcare is discussed in Chapter Six.

How Do I Find a Shared Household to Join? Is It Possible to Start My Own?

Some households can be contacted through national publications or organizations, although your best bet is probably a local community information center. Since groups are often able to pick-and-choose among a number of candidates for membership, being clear about the kind of commune you want to join will improve your chances of being chosen. You may not find an existing group that fits your needs, or you may already know some friends with whom you would like to start a household. There is nothing to stop you from getting some people together to discuss the formation of a new commune. To find out whether you are sufficiently compatible to live together, you can discuss some key questions, including how much closeness you expect, how housekeeping tasks will be accomplished, whether children will be included, and what childrearing methods will be used. If you make a tentative decision to form a household it is possible to conduct a trial run by going camping together or by renting a house for a limited time.

Finding a commune to join and starting a new commune are the subjects discussed in Chapter Seven, which includes a helpful checklist for interviewers and interviewees. Appendix D describes another method of founding a household — the owner of the house recruits people to live there communally.

What Happens If Someone Moves Out or If the Group Disbands?

Commune members don't vow to remain together for life. They leave when they are dissatisfied with the group, when they accept a better job in another city, or when they want to live alone with someone they have fallen in love with. A member's departure can cause emotional strain, but this strain is alleviated when people talk openly about why the member is going. Then comes the task of finding a replacement member. Fortunately, communal households have worked out fairly effective methods of recruiting candidates, screening them for compatibility with the group, and selecting the most promising candidate. If a commune no longer meets the needs of the group as a whole, it disbands. Groups almost always disband in orderly fashion.

Chapter Eight is devoted to membership turnover and disbanding.

What Legal and Real Estate Questions Must Be Resolved When a Group Rents or Buys a Communal House?

The main legal question concerns discriminatory zoning ordinances that are in force in some communities. These ordinances limit the number of unrelated persons who may live together. Within a metropolitan area, some communities may have discriminatory zoning while others do not. Therefore, before renting or buying, it is wise to investigate local zoning rules. Groups that want to rent a house are in a more favorable position today because landlords have warmed up to communes and in some instances actively court them. Groups that rent are well advised to write up a brief agreement among themselves specifying, among other things, who holds the lease and what happens if a member leaves.

Many communal groups own their house. There are advantages to home ownership, but, whether you are a traditional family or a communal one, home buying isn't something to rush into without planning. Groups must decide what type of legal entity they will create to hold the title to their house, then draft an ownership agreement that spells out who the owners are, how shares can be transferred, who pays for maintenance, and so on. Communes whose members hold regular jobs should have no difficulty obtaining a real estate loan. But they may have to shop around to obtain homeowner's insurance at a reasonable rate.

A special situation is created when a communal house is owned by just one member of the group, or by a couple who are members. If the rights of the owner and of the other members are agreed upon at the outset, "landlord-tenant" conflicts can be avoided. A particular formula for selection of members and payment of rent has been used successfully in a number of these "single-owner" houses.

Legal and real estate matters and the special case of the single-owner household are all elaborated in the appendices.

Now you have an overview of this book. If a chapter takes up a question of special interest to you, you can turn to it directly. If you want the full picture, the next chapter details the variety of communes available.

2. TYPES OF SHARED HOUSEHOLDS

In *Future Shock*, published in 1970, Alvin Toffler foresaw the imminent emergence of communal households. "The goals," he wrote, "may be social, religious, political, even recreational. Thus we shall before long begin to see communal families of surfers dotting the beaches of California and Southern France, if they don't already." Toffler also foresaw communes built around businesses. "Instead of a communal farm, why not a computer software company whose program writers live and work communally?" he asked. "Why not an education technology company whose members pool their money and merge their families?"

By so speculating, Toffler joined a distinguished company of authors who have proposed other visions of communal utopia. Plato is often credited with being first. *The Republic* had 5,040 citizens. Only those of the "best stock" were encouraged to have children, who were brought up in a state nursery. Sir Thomas More coined the word "utopia," deriving it from two Greek words. His *Utopia* was a crescent-shaped island where there was no private property and no money. Aldous Huxley's *Island* had inhabitants who drank a psychedelic drug and could change jobs whenever they got bored. The islanders eliminated competition, controlled their population, and enjoyed constant plenty. These are only three of the many imaginary utopias described in literature.

The purpose of this book is not to imagine utopias that may or may not work in actual practice or to propose communes that haven't been tried. Instead this book limits itself to descriptions of actual communes and seeks to explain what makes them work. So the types described in this chapter are limited to communes that already exist. But I don't want to imply that additional types will not be invented or would not work. If you're interested in inventing a new type of commune, this chapter might be a good place to start, because it points out some of the difficulties associated with each of the existing types. Armed with the knowledge that, for example, lack of interdependence is a hazard in cluster communities, or that too intense interaction can "burn out" the members of a growth household, you can do a better job of creating a new type of commune that avoids these problems.

The types of communes described in this chapter are based primarily on the purposes groups have for living together. For example, in the family household and the single-parents' household, childrearing is a central concern. A particular interest—say in the arts or in politics—unites members of the shared-interest household. Members of an elders' household want to avoid the social isolation of old age, while members of a vacation-retirement household are planning ahead for the day when they will be old. A cluster community seeks to combine some advantages of communal living with greater privacy than communal living affords. The growth household is started by people who are enthusiastic about personal growth.

No classification system is perfect. Classifying individuals into types is always misleading, since each individual is unique. So it is with communes; composed of unique individuals, no two households are exactly alike. A household that is predominantly one type always has some characteristics of other types. Some households are such a mix of characteristics that it's hard to say which type predominates. But though the single-purpose household is nonexistent the categories are useful, because people who are interested in communal living need a way of thinking about the kind of commune they might like to create or join.

SHARED HOUSEHOLDS
CLASSIFIED BY PURPOSE

The Family Household

This type of commune is most often founded by families who have children and who want to create the richest possible domestic life—a life centered around the kids, the kitchen, and the garden. In this description, Dennis Jaffe captures the flavor of one family household in suburban Connecticut:

> The entrance leads to the nerve center of the house, the huge kitchen and pantry area. Pots are usually steaming on both stoves, cooking dinner, yogurt, and maybe dye for cloth; there is usually bread baking in the oven or cooling on the side. The large table is full of papers, magazines, adults and kids. Notes all over the cupboards carry messages, announcements, job rosters, menus, guests expected. This is where people hang out, from the first coffee at six A.M. until after midnight.

This commune was started by four middle-aged couples and a divorced woman who invested twenty thousand dollars each as the downpayment on a suburban estate. These adults brought with them their fourteen children. Family households exist in the city as well as in the suburbs: One group of three married couples with small children bought a three-story home in Berkeley, near the University of California, to house their families.

Two kinds of family households have been identified

by Jane Ferrar, a sociologist who was part of a team of researchers, headed by Professor Benjamin Zablocki of Columbia University, that spent two years studying sixty-five communal households in six major cities. The multiple-family household is formed by two or more families, each of which has children. The central-family household is formed by one family with children which owns a large house and recruits single people to share it.

The multiple-family household. Parents living in this type of commune said almost unanimously that their households were good places to bring up children. The main problem they encountered was getting all the parents to agree on childrearing methods. Philosophies of childrearing can vary considerably from one family to the next. What kids should eat, how much TV they should watch, how late they should stay up—these are a few of the issues that parents can disagree about. One advantage of the multiple-family household is that all of the adults are accustomed to living with children. One mother who lives in such a household says, "I can tolerate the little kids that aren't mine because I know my kids are making the same racket and making the same mess. No one can blame sticky fingers all over the place on any one set of children, because there are five sets of sticky little fingers going all the time."

The central-family household. Families living in this kind of commune also reported that their households were good places to raise kids. With only one set of parents present, conflicts over childrearing style were greatly diminished. The main problem in this kind of household is that the married couple, by virtue of seniority and ownership of the house, tends to control both the childrearing and other aspects of communal life. The single members often resent not being equal members of the commune and sometimes move out for this reason. Another difficulty is that parents sometimes have trouble recruiting single adults who are fond enough of small children to live with the noise and mess they create.

Children reared in family households are emotionally healthy. A question of concern to parents is how living communally will affect their children. Several researchers have concluded that communally reared children tend to mature early, to be unusually independent and self-assured, and to be exceptionally competent in relationships with other people. Sociologist Rosabeth Kanter headed a team of social scientists which studied parents and children in thirty-five middle-class communes in Boston and New Haven. Although the average group had ten members of all ages, the researchers found that the children were not confused or frightened by the necessity of dealing with adults other than their parents. Kanter found that they

> learn to make choices and learn to express themselves easily to grown-ups. . . . The enlarged size and complexity of the households mean that children have to learn to "speak up" in order to be heard, to be persuasive and interpersonally skilled in order to get something they want.

Communal living is a learning and growing experience for kids as much as for adults. Even small children, Kanter found, "develop a noticeable ease in relating to other people, needing minimal guidance."

Sterling Alam, a researcher at the University of Illinois, reached a similar conclusion after intensively studying one household formed by three married couples and their seven children. Two husbands in this group were college professors; the third was a minister. Alam reported "two outstanding conclusions: that the children developed a marked degree of independence, initiative, and self-assurance; and that they learned to relate well to all adults, not just their own parents."

Two more researchers, Larry and Joan Constantine, studied children in group-marriage households scattered across the country. A group marriage is a special kind of commune in which sexual relationships cross couple lines. This meant that the kids were living in households that depart much more radically from the nuclear-family norm than the communes described in this book. Even so, the Constantines discovered that most of these children were highly independent, had positive self-images, and were "confident, healthy, in-touch kids."

These studies of communal children all point to the same conclusion: Today's isolated nuclear families are only one place to rear kids. Children reared in households that resemble old-fashioned extended familes may grow up to be more emotionally healthy adults than if they had been reared in nuclear families.

Families in adult-oriented communes. One question Jane Ferrar investigated was what type of communal household provides the best setting for family life. Some of the parents she studied had blundered into households where the other members had no interest in children. For example, there was a husband who persuaded his wife to move into a large house with a bunch of fraternity buddies. The husband's friends teased the kids, refused to help clean up after them, and even forgot to store sharp objects out of their reach. Families are better off living in a commune where everyone likes kids and where childrearing is a central purpose for the group's existence, not an afterthought.

Communal childrearing is also discussed in other sections of this book. Chapter Three explains that parents lose some control over their children when they live communally, and they normally view this as a blessing. In Chapter Three, concerned parents can also read about how nonparents who love children are selected for membership in a family household and how children can be more fully included in the life of a group. Chapter Five discusses the importance of having children participate in house meetings Chapter Six explains how parents accommodate differences in childrearing styles and how children participate in communal housekeeping. Chapter Eight discusses the impact of membership turnover on children.

The Single-Parents' Household

Single parents who come together to live communally want to replace the emotional and economic trials of raising children alone with a better way of life in a group that resembles a big, old-fashioned family. "We're together because it is so much better than any possible alternative," says one of three single parents who share a house in Oakland, California. "If we abandoned this household, where would we go? The idea of being a single parent living alone is absolutely wretched to all of us." By pooling their financial resources, single parents can afford to rent or buy a house suitable for family living.

They can also pool emotional resources. "I have a lot of companionship and caring here," says a single mother who lives communally. "I have a real home base and genuine friendships and real closeness that has nothing to do with sex. Because I don't get lonely, I'm not driven into sexual relationships that I don't want." Communal living has improved her relationship with her eight-year-old daughter. "It isn't continously just the two of us," she explains. "My daughter gets eight other people to relate to, so she isn't always coming to me to get all her needs met. I don't feel a continuous need to entertain her or be with her. This means that when we are together I really want to be with her."

This mother is one of two single parents in her household. Although none of the other members has children, they all like kids, and the arrangement works well for everyone. Some single parents are less fortunate. They have trouble finding a communal household that will accept them and their children. But single parents can join together and form their own commune.

The Oakland commune was begun by three divorced parents in their thirties who had custody of seven children ranging in age from four to twelve. The parents were Gerald, thirty-two, a computer-time salesman; Susan, thirty-four, an unemployed teacher receiving aid to families with dependent children; and Frank, thirty-five, a certified public accountant. Gerald and Susan had met a few years earlier when both were married. While they were considering the idea of forming a commune, Susan met Frank at a Parents Without Partners party and recruited him. It was difficult to find a landlord who would rent to people with seven kids, but eventually the trio leased a two-story frame house with a four-room cottage in the back. "We felt strongly that everyone should have a measure of privacy, so each adult has a separate room, and no child has to share a room with more than one other kid," Susan says.

Because she was home during the day, there was initially a tendency to cast her in the housewife-and-mother role. "Part of this even came from me," she says, "because I had been a housewife for a long time and I was in the habit of picking up around the house. But I was able to say to the guys, 'Now look here; you are not supporting me, I do not owe you a maid service.'" Since then everyone has recognized the need to distribute the work equally. The three adults take turns cleaning the common rooms. Susan always cooks, and the two men are permanent dishwashers and kitchen clean-up crew. Sometimes a baby-sitter is hired, but when someone goes out at night, another parent usually agrees to put the absent parent's kids to bed.

"We think of ourselves as an extended family, or as a good blend of independent families and shared community," Gerald says. It is important to all three parents that their special bonds with their own children remain intact: "The kids understand that we're the Brooms and the Ogilvies and the Cerasis merged into one large family," says Susan. "And there's always an affinity to the parent proper. But at the same time there's a real closeness among the children and the other adults. The children refer to each other as sisters and brothers, which is not something we encouraged. They just did it."

The Shared-Interest Household

Members of this type of commune share common interests. For example, one recently formed household is composed of people interested in healing, body work, and astrology. Another group was formed by musicians who jam together after dinner. Some shared-interest households are started by vegetarians who choose to live with others who share their diet and outlook on life. Often a shared-interest commune is an offshoot of a community organization. For example, a number of households have been created by parents and teachers active in the same alternative school. Another common type is the commune formed by people who share an interest in a particular kind of politics.

"We have a common political perspective which is expressed in our newspaper, *Issues in Radical Therapy*," says psychologist Claude Steiner of the eight-member Berkeley household he lives in. "This common perspective gives us projects to get together over and something in common to talk about. Communal living makes it possible to live on much less money so that people can put some of their efforts into improving their lives and fighting the system, instead of working forty hours a week and having no energy for anything else." Because the focus in this household is on political work and on psychotherapy, members often hold evening meetings at the house. The newspaper is put together at the house, but there is no requirement that all members participate. Some work on the paper and some don't.

The stereotyped image of a political commune is that of a humorless group single-mindedly devoted to its goal. But a political household need not be anything like that. A group of college friends who had been active in the same radical causes decided to live together a few years after graduation. Their household is lively and full of humor. "Our favorite topics are therapy, radical politics, the vagaries of personal relationships, sex, each other, and what everyone is up to," says a member. "There's a great deal of sassing, of kidding that goes on all the time. It's very nice, very familyish. Siblingish." No political fanatic would coin a word like siblingish.

Sometimes, though, a shared-interest household does attract doctrinaire people. When this happens there is a risk of internal conflict between people who consider themselves "more committed" to the shared interest and other members who are criticized for being less involved. One way to avert this kind of conflict is to select as members people who are tolerant rather than doctrinaire. Another useful precaution is to reach agreement on whether members will be expected to participate in projects together. Otherwise there can be conflict between those who expected that everyone would pitch in to work on the newspaper or help out at the alternative school or give benefit concerts and those who thought that such projects would be optional.

The Multi-Interest Household

If the shared-interest household is an exciting place to live because of what people have in common, the multi-interest household is exciting because of what the members *don't* have in common. One household, for instance, is composed of a dancer, a lawyer, a woman who works part-time as a musician and part-time as a motorcycle mechanic, and three writers. One of the writers gets all the magazine article ideas he needs at home. "I get more stimulation and I hear more stories than I could ever possibly use," he says happily. But this group of three men and three women (aged twenty-eight to thirty-four) thrives on stimulation. If the conversation lags, they show movies in the living room.

A former member of another multi-interest household remembers it like this:

Everybody in the house was different. It ranged from me

doing political community organizing to a physicist doing some ozone layer thing. We also had a gardener, a journalist, an astronomer, and a hardware store employee who did Hebrew translations on the side. We had dinner together and we could get drunk together and play fifty songs on the piano. We respected each other, we communicated about what was going on, and we knew a lot about each other. There was a definite closeness, even though everyone had close friends outside the house. It was marvelous, a really educational experience.

As she implies, members of a multi-interest household rejoice in their diversity. They value the opportunity to learn from others they might never encounter in the normal course of their lives, let alone get to know well. Because care is taken to recruit open-minded people who respect different points of view, members of a multi-interest household are able to share insights and experiences born of diverse backgrounds and occupations. Because members are not expected to have any particular interest or viewpoint, there is no risk of attracting doctrinaire members or of instigating conflict over which member is "more committed" to a shared interest. Still, there are limits to the value differences that members of any commune can accept. Chapter Seven explains how to check in advance for extreme differences that might make living together unwise.

The excitement of the multi-interest household derives from differences, but it is possible to carry this idea too far. I know one person who resolved to start a commune and deliberately sought diverse and unusual people to join him. One of these interesting people built an ornamental fountain in his room. Real water flowed through the fountain, and one day it sprang a leak and flooded two floors of the house. Another member retreated to his room to smoke marijuana and burn incense. One night he fell asleep and the incense fell over, starting a fire that destroyed part of the attic. One lesson the group learned from these experiences is that it isn't necessary to seek out people who are "different" to live with. As everyone who lives communally quickly finds out, we're all different. So simply selecting people you like will almost always produce a healthy measure of diversity.

The Living-Working Household

This is the kind of commune that Alvin Toffler envisioned when he suggested the creation of a computer software company whose program writers live and work together or an education technology company whose employees merge their families. A few years ago, David and Elena French traveled across the country searching for communes that combined living and working. They found only a handful and described them in their book *Working Communally.*

The Good Times Commune is one such group, formed in 1969 to publish *Good Times*, a San Francisco underground newspaper. When the paper folded in 1972, the commune members used their graphic-arts skills to support themselves. Today all members of the group, plus a few outsiders, participate in the communal business of illustration, design, layout, pasteup, camera copy and darkroom work, and typesetting. As befits a commune, organization of the business is nonhierarchical. Members attempt to live and work in accordance with their social and political values, spelled out in a "social contract" renegotiated every six months or whenever a new member joins. A new member who doesn't possess graphic-arts skills is expected to contribute to the communal income by at first taking a job with "some other nonhierarchical group."

Some living-working groups are able to put all new members to work immediately because their business doesn't require a high skill level. One such commune operates a telephone answering service; the members installed a switchboard on their enclosed front porch and only have to commute that far to work. Other groups have started restaurants, and one commune demolishes buildings and recycles the used building materials at a profit.

But what about Toffler's vision of a high-technology commune? This is a challenging idea. It would be necessary to unite people who have compatible personal values, the right technical skills, and the interpersonal skills needed to cooperate effectively at work and at home. Many potential members who met one or two requirements for joining would have to be rejected because they failed to meet the third. Turnover, which seems to be inevitable in communes, becomes increasingly difficult to deal with when replacement members must possess exacting qualifications. Imagine advertising for a likable person with a marketing background and at least two years' experience programming in Fortran, who doesn't smoke, has no children, and wants to live communally and work in a business run by consensus! Despite these difficulties, it should be possible to put together a high-technology living-working group, although I don't believe anyone has done it yet.

Social critics have argued that Americans lead lonely, fragmented lives because we work in one place with one group of people and come home to a different place and another group of people. The living-working group eliminates this fragmentation. But members of these groups report that unfragmented relationships can become uncomfortably intense because so much time is spent together. Sometimes members take frequent vacations to reduce this intensity.

Another hazard of the living-working group is the temptation to set overambitious goals. For example, one group of friends who wanted to create "a greater synthesis of work and play and life" moved into a ramshackle three-story house and began to rebuild it while simultaneously launching several small businesses. At the end of two years, two of the businesses had failed, the household was wracked with dissension, and the group fell apart. Surveying the disaster, the former members concluded that they might have succeeded by seeking to achieve only one or two major goals at a time.

The Elders' Household

Nobody looks forward to growing old in a nursing home. But how about growing old surrounded by friends and people with similar interests and experiences in a familylike household where members control their own lives? This idea is being tried out in a number of cities. In Lakewood, Colorado, outside Denver, six people aged fifty-six and older share a six-bedroom, split-level suburban home. In Baltimore, three suburban communes are each home to five elderly people. Four similar households exist in Washington, D.C., and in Delaware. In Evanston, Illinois, a dozen elderly people live in six interconnecting townhouses. Ten "autonomous families" of elderly people belong to the nonprofit Share-A-Home Association headquartered in Winter Park, Florida. These communal families, with between eight and twenty members, are located in Florida, Ohio, North Carolina, and Georgia. In late 1978 a new group was being formed in Kentucky.

All of these elders' households are sponsored by a nonprofit agency, most often a religious one (Share-A-Home is an independent organization that receives some assistance from religious groups). Each commune has at least a part-time staff of one or more assistants who do some of the cooking, perform the heavy housework, and drive members to the doctor's office. This doesn't mean, however, that life in these groups is anything like life in a nursing home.

In the Share-A-Home communes, for example, the members are definitely in charge. They can hire and fire the staff and they vote new members into the house. They do as much cooking as they wish, do some of the housework, and contribute their favorite pieces of furniture to the household. "The family pays the staff to be their servants," says Jim Gillies, who founded Share-

A-Home in 1969. Because members enjoy a measure of control over their lives, they keep their self-respect. As Jess Bush, eighty-five, told a visitor: "Some of the members of the family are forgetful sometimes, but here we don't think of it as senility, as they do in nursing homes. We really don't have difficulties with things like that here. Everyone forgets something sometimes, but we don't mind."

Sponsored elders' households seem to be succeeding well. The next step will come when older people start their own communes, without sponsor or staff. Grassroots alliances of older people are working toward this goal in San Francisco and Philadelphia, and as this book went to press the Shared Living Project in Boston was selecting fifteen older people to move into a three-story nineteenth-century townhouse equipped with an elevator. Plans called for the house to have a resident manager during the first year and for a residents' council to take over thereafter. The house was purchased by the Back Bay Aging Concerns Committee, primarily with money obtained from foundations. (The San Francisco, Philadelphia, and Boston households are listed in Appendix A.)

Although many older people view communal living as a promising alternative, they don't always find it easy making a transition to a new lifestyle late in life. The transition is smoother when an elderly person has already had experience living communally before retirement. This is the idea behind the vacation-retirement household, which serves its members first as a vacation retreat, then as a permanent home.

The Vacation-Retreat Household

In 1971, three families from New York's Westchester County and one family from Delaware came together to buy a historic thirty-three room mansion called Grasmere. Located in Rhinebeck, one hundred miles north of New York City, the estate includes twenty-five acres of woods and parkland. The Georgian mansion has fourteen-foot ceilings and seven master bedrooms. The founders of this commune include a psychologist, a psychiatrist, a partner in a market research organization, and a schoolteacher. Two more families joined the group in the years after its founding, bringing the membership to ten middle-aged adults and twelve children ranging in age from eleven to young adulthood. In 1978, the group announced that it wanted to recruit one or two additional families.

Only a caretaker lives at Grasmere all year. The families spend vacations at the estate, learning by experience how to live together communally. They also devote much time to restoring the mansion—in one bathroom, eighteen people painted in shifts from morning to night. But there is also time to swim, hike, and fish—all on their own land—and to enjoy communal meals. The teenagers even produce a newspaper, the *Grasmere Gazette*. Adults and children participate together in house meetings. But the commune's vacation phase is only the beginning.

"Our focus is on living in an extended family group during our middle years and on learning the interpersonal skills necessary to build a lasting commume," the members have explained. "Our long-range view is toward the possibility of living communally in retirement." All of the members have friends or relatives who grew lonely and isolated in old age. If Grasmere's retirement phase succeeds, the members will grow old enjoying abundant companionship and the support of close friends.

The Men's Household

I don't know of any communes started by men who wanted to live together primarily for political reasons. Most members of men's households are gay, and they want the emotional support that gay people can give one another.

The members of one Berkeley household are not gay,

they are bisexual. Their commune was founded in 1976 when two men leased a house that had survived the 1906 earthquake and advertised for more bisexuals to join them. Three female members were recruited but quickly moved on. For nearly two years all six members of the group were male. "We had to do all the things that men aren't taught to do, like wash dishes and keep a kitchen clean, cook meals, and sew on buttons," says Tom, one of the members. "And even more important, we had to be warm and sharing with one another rather than being totally dependent on women for emotional support." The men succeeded, largely because theirs is a household that values these traits. The members have been active in men's groups and recently helped to publish a resource directory for men against sexism.

Aside from showing that men can live communally without women, this household demonstrates that members of a sexual minority can support each other by living communally. "Because I am bisexual, I am threatening to both the heterosexual community and the homosexual community," Tom says. "I spent a lot of my years trying to fit into one or the other of those communities and never feeling welcome in either. When I saw the ad for a bisexual household, I thought it would be exactly what I wanted, and it was." This is no longer an all-male group. In 1978, two men moved out and were replaced by two bisexual women.

The Women's Household

All members of a women's household are female, but women's communes are started for different reasons. Some are begun by active feminists who view living communally with other women as a social and political act. Others are formed by single mothers who see living with other mothers as a good way to rear children. Still others are started by lesbians who want the companionship and emotional support of living with women who fully accept them and their sexual orientation.

Bonsilene House in Woodmont, Connecticut, was

founded in 1972 by five young women who were active in feminist politics and community work. Two more women joined later, and in 1976 the group purchased the house, which up to then had been rented. Having grown up in a world that conditioned them to be passive and to be dependent on men, these women saw living together as a way to do something on their own, to achieve independence from men, to get support from women friends, and to develop their own identities. Their house meetings sometimes resembled consciousness-raising sessions as members exchanged life histories and sought to understand how sex roles had shaped their experience. At last report, the group had decided for unspecified reasons to admit a male feminist. "The conception of Bonsilene as a 'women's house' will change," the members believed, "but the struggle for collective, nonsexist growth will not."

A group of somewhat older women formed a household in the San Francisco Bay area the same year Bonsilene was founded. The California women had already achieved independence from men—most were living alone when they decided to start the commune, and some were lesbians. These women were attracted to the companionship and economy of communal living, and all were interested in the women's movement, which sometimes gave them common projects to participate in. Over six years this group has evolved into a close-knit family of women. "We do all the normal things that families do," a member explains. "We take vacations together, celebrate each other's birthdays, take care of each other when we're sick, and lend each other money. We even entertain each other's relatives."

The Growth Household

This type of commune is based in the personal growth or human potential movement. People who start a growth household have experienced the aliveness and the closeness with others which encounter groups or other kinds of growth groups generate. By living together, they hope to make this aliveness and closeness part of daily life. Frequently they also wish to achieve greater self-understanding and self-acceptance and to learn how to communicate better and have more satisfactory relationships with other people.

Family therapist Dennis Jaffe describes one group that held encounter-style meetings, sometimes several times a week. The main purpose was to overcome sexist attitudes. After a year all members felt they had been through "a tremendous growth experience." Jaffe studied another group that held frequent encounter meetings and reported that the members "have all learned to be open to their feelings and to use others for feedback and support." Both communes gave up encountering during the second year when the members felt that it was no longer necessary and had become too emotionally draining and too time consuming. Communes built on an encounter group model tend to "burn out" in this way. Then the group either lowers the level of emotional interaction or disbands.

It is possible to build a growth household on a communication model rather than an encounter model. Harwood House in Oakland is an example. All members have been involved in growth groups of various kinds, either as leaders or participants. At the weekly house meetings they sit group fashion in a circle on the living room rug. These meetings are modeled after groups in which people practice communication skills. Members do not attack one another in hopes of stirring powerful bursts of emotion. Instead the meetings are unusually quiet, with great emphasis placed on careful listening and making sure that everyone's feelings are understood and respected. This seems to be a more enduring model for a growth commune; Harwood House, for example, has functioned successfully for more than five years.

The Luxury Household

Picture the luxuries that could be enjoyed by eight or ten people who combined their incomes in a common search for a more affluent lifestyle. To begin with they could buy an estate. That should leave enough money to buy a motorhome and take trips together. After saving up for another year or two, they could buy a vacation home or a yacht—and so on. It may sound wonderful in theory, but I don't know of any such group actually in existence in this country. Grasmere, the New York estate, might qualify as a luxury household, but the members are motivated by more than the desire to accumulate possessions. Their most important purpose is to learn how to live communally so that they will have people to share their lives with in retirement.

Still, some people are interested in the idea of a commune where the central purpose would be to live luxuriously. Through the University of California's Extension Division, a weekend workshop was given for people intrigued by middle-class communes. The 165 participants filled out questionnaires that showed some liked the thought of living in a commune that would be luxurious, have a high degree of privacy, and be highly organized and controlled by many rules. The difficulty with this arrangement is that those who envisioned it weren't interested in interacting closely with other people. The workshop leaders, organizational behavior expert David Bradford and psychologist Simon Klevansky, note that the vision of an affluent commune actually resembled a club formed by people who want to own a boat or airplane jointly. Because they were unable to find any existing commune where the guiding purpose was luxury living, Bradford and Klevansky suggest that the idea occurs to people who have just begun to think about communal living and who soon realize that their vision is too narrow. Then they abandon the idea of living communally or expand it so that family or community becomes the purpose for living together, with luxury seen as a fringe benefit.

There may not be any luxury households in this country, but I do know of a semiluxurious one in Britain. Philip Abrams and Andrew McCulloch, two English sociologists who wrote about this commune, call it Hillside, because the manor house is situated just below the top of a ridge. Trees surround the house on three sides and on the fourth there are wide views of some of the most beautiful rolling countryside in England. Below the house are the tennis courts, terraced flower gardens, coach house, and other outbuildings. The origin of this commune goes back to a group of boys who became friends at public school (as the English call their upper-class boarding schools) and lived together in flats as university students. These friends became interested in communal living after their university days. They divided the country into sections, systematically viewing every estate offered for sale. Eventually they settled on Hillside and four people agreed to invest twenty thousand pounds as the downpayment. But the group was not affluent enough to limit membership to the core group of friends. To make the mortgage payments, they were obliged to recruit more people, and the membership eventually reached twenty-four.

The original decision to live in communal luxury thus dictated the large size of the group, and the commune's history can be seen largely as an attempt to deal with so many people. When the members realized that the size of their group prevented them from living with a minimum of rules and organization and even from getting to know one another well, they decided to form three households within the commune. There were two kitchens in the house and a third in the coach house, and this made it possible to divide into three groups of about eight members each. Each group was named after the color of its kitchen. Most members of Yellow Kitchen shared an interest in the women's movement and got along well. But the members of Blue Kitchen were not compatible and their number rapidly dwindled to two. The third group remained together but ate separately, a practice viewed as less than communal.

That was the commune's condition when the sociologists ended their study, although they noted that the members were continuing vigorous efforts to achieve a more perfect communal life. Because Hillside grew out of remarkably enduring friendships, it clearly is more than just a scheme to live luxuriously. Hillside demonstrates that people who dream of living together in a luxurious commune can turn their dream into reality— although, of course, the reality may not match up exactly with the original dream.

SHARED HOUSEHOLDS CLASSIFIED BY SIZE AND SEX BALANCE

There are other ways to classify shared households than by purpose. The simplest approach is to say, "There are two kinds: large households and small ones." Actually this classification scheme isn't as silly as it sounds. Regardless of what type it is, a commune's size helps determine what living there is like. A second factor that affects life in any commune, regardless of type, is the ratio of male and female members.

Large or Small: Pros and Cons

Most communal households range in size from four or five members to a dozen or so. Both large and small groups have advantages and disadvantages. Larger groups are more economical. If you have ten members, a three-hundred-dollar dryer costs thirty dollars each; if you have only four members, the cost is seventy-five dollars each. Larger groups are also more efficient. If ten people live communally, each person may be required to cook only once every two weeks and may have only one housekeeping chore. Reduce the number of people to four or five, and each person may have to cook each week and perform several chores. Larger groups provide more constant companionship — there is almost always someone willing to engage in conversation, start a minor project, or go to the movies. More interests and occupations are represented in a larger group. There are more personal crises and triumphs to share, and more intellectual stimulation.

One disadvantage of the larger group is that people must live in a more organized fashion. A member of one ten-person household that includes five small children says, "Because we're so many people, we have to be organized or go under. We've got to have places and spaces for things and things have got to be put away." Most large groups are organized in additional ways. Usually they have a wall chart in the kitchen showing when each member will cook and shop and what chores they will do. Members of a small household can make most of their decisions informally, perhaps over dinner. Larger groups usually find that formal house meetings are necessary to coordinate activities and to clear up misunderstandings.

Coordination becomes time consuming in a larger group. House meetings in one San Francisco commune of more than a dozen people sometimes lasted until midnight. Eventually the group decided to reduce its size by not replacing members who moved out. This isn't to say that members of smaller households escape the necessity of coordinating their activities or of communicating clearly with one another. Chapters Four and Five show that coordination and communication are important aspects of life in any communal household. But these two tasks do grow more demanding as size increases.

Male-Female Ratios

Most middle-class communes attempt to balance the number of men and women in the group (except, of course, the groups composed of all women or all men). But suppose there are seven bedrooms: Then the issue to be resolved in a house meeting is do we have three women and four men, or four men and three women?

There are three reasons that groups usually strive for a sex balance. As I said in Chapter One, a communal household offers an unusual opportunity to establish genuine friendships with the opposite sex — friendships that don't depend on sexual involvement. When there are equal numbers of men and women, opportunities for this kind of friendship are the greatest.

The second reason that groups aim for a sex balance is that neither sex likes to feel outnumbered. Women and men usually want to have members of the same sex in the group for emotional support and to share their interests.

The final reason for having a sex balance is the desire to have both "male" and "female" traits and abilities in the group. At first both these traits may be firmly divided: Women tend to be more nurturing, and men often know how to fix things around the house or how to deal with the landlord or the bank lending officer. A household functions more effectively when it draws on both male and female abilities. But an advantage of communal living is that it helps people transcend sex roles. Because of the stress on sharing work equally, everyone gets to learn how to cook, clean, work in the yard, pay bills, and deal with officials. Men even learn to be more nurturing because communal living requires them to understand others better.

THE CLUSTER COMMUNITY

The cluster community is not a shared household. It is an attempt to achieve the kind of closeness that develops in communes without any loss of privacy. Thus a small apartment building may be taken over by a group with the goal of starting a community. The members can share meals, childcare, projects, and leisure time—but they have their self-contained living units to retreat to when they want privacy. In Los Angeles, a group of families with small children bought a garden apartment building. They hired a teacher and started their own daycare center in the building. A cluster community can also take the form of private suburban homes grouped together.

The cluster's weak point is the very feature that makes it so attractive—the ability of the members to withdraw to the privacy of their own units or homes. In a commune, such total withdrawal from the group isn't possible. A high degree of interdependence is built into a communal household because the members use the same kitchen, dining room, living room, and bathrooms. Members can withdraw temporarily to the privacy of their own rooms—but when they emerge, interaction is automatic. Because interaction isn't automatic in a cluster, there is a risk that people will spend too much time in their self-contained quarters and that the hoped-for community will fail to grow.

In the fall of 1970, seven families who belonged to Valley United Church in California resolved to create a small community that would have the feel of an extended family. Recruiting several more families to join what they called New Community One, they purchased fifteen acres in Orinda, a San Francisco suburb, and sought county approval for a planned unit development that would have grouped their single-family homes on four acres, leaving the remaining land as open space. Neighbors waged a costly three-year legal battle against the proposal and won. Each family was forced to build on a separate half-acre lot. However, by mid-1976, a half-dozen homes, each costing around one hundred thousand dollars, had been finished. By the fall of 1978 the development was almost complete, with only two of the planned fourteen houses still unbuilt.

But the hoped-for extended family feeling never materialized. "The dream that we had looks as if it's not possible," says William O. Smith, the person who invested the most time and effort in the struggle to make New Community One a reality. He traces much of the problem to the uphill zoning fight. Many families dropped out when they could no longer afford to build, because the development plan that finally won approval was more costly. Additional couples dropped out when their marriages failed. Only two of the families originally involved in planning New Community One live there today. True, it was possible to recruit new families gradually as the original ones dropped out — the beautiful building sites on a gently rolling hillside made that easy — but the newcomers lacked the enthusiasm for community that had inspired the original group. When the time came to build the recreation building and swimming pool that had been planned as a focus for the community, four families refused to contribute and the plan was abandoned. Regular potluck dinners had been held in the early days, but some of the newcomers didn't like the idea, preferring to let gatherings occur spontaneously. None did. Once the early enthusiasm for community had waned, the architectural plan — detached single-family homes — made it impossible to revive. "Most families have given first loyalty to their individual piece of real estate," Smith says. "It's just a nice suburban neighborhood."

Where New Community One apparently has failed, another cluster has succeeded. In 1971, a group of families who belonged to the Old Cambridge Baptist Church in Cambridge, Massachusetts, decided to buy an apartment building, naming it Common Place. "We ran into each other at church meetings and that was fun and enjoyable and made us want to spend more time together, but with people spread out all over the Boston metropolitan area it wasn't possible," says Jim Stockard, a Common Place founder. "Living together also made sense economically and ecologically. For example, we have four washers and dryers hooked up in the basement and all twelve families use them instead of having twelve washers and dryers." The three-story twelve-unit building is shaped like an H. There are frequent picnics in the big backyard. A number of members have active green thumbs, and motorists stop to admire the profusion of flowers which surrounds the building. Twenty-one adults, all in the thirty-to-forty age range, and thirteen children live here. The fathers' occupations are solidly middle-class: there are three housing consultants, an accountant, several high school teachers, the church secretary, and a state official. Three single women and one unmarried couple belong; all the other couples are married.

The extended family feeling that didn't happen at New Community One is quite evident at Common Place. Members eat together spontaneously as often as once a week. Childcare is shared as a matter of course — parents who decide to see a movie on the spur of the moment feel free to leave their kids with another parent, for example. Twice a year everyone goes on a communal retreat in the country to renew friendships. Because of a remodeling project that joined two apartments, two nuclear families now live communally.

Several factors account for the success of Common Place. The building was purchased within a year of the original decision to live together, so there was no time for members to drop out or for the original enthusiasm for community to die. Because members live in the same building, rather than in separate houses, a measure of sharing is inevitable. To ensure greater interdependence, the group is organized as a cooperative instead of as a condominium. Condominium apartments are owned individually, but in a cooperative members own shares in the building as a whole. All of the work of running the building —from cleaning, landscaping, and

maintenance to budgeting and paying taxes — is
handled by the members. A five-person board does the
planning. Membership rotates each year, so no member
serves a second time until everyone has served once.

Another reason that Common Place became a community is the religious faith of the members. Their religious studies gave them a clearer understanding of the
isolation that many nuclear families live in today and
strengthened their conviction that it was possible to
overcome this isolation. Common Place has its own
"house church" that meets once a month for study,
worship, or celebration. About 70 percent of the residents attend these meetings.

People who lack a religious commitment could create a
successful cluster community. The crucial consideration
would be to structure the community so that interdependence is built in. A plan that would create an
interdependent community while preserving family privacy has been sketched by David Bradford and his wife,
Eva. The Bradfords envision a suburban cluster built to
order. An architectural plan shows six duplexes that
would provide each family with private living quarters of
two to four rooms depending on the number of children.
The duplexes radiate from a central building that houses
a communal dining hall and a "childcare and play facility
. . . lounge and recreational areas, small TV lounges . . . a
game room . . . possibly a gymnasium . . . laundry . . .
and a shop, darkroom, and pottery and art studios as the
need for them develops." Because members would eat
together and engage in recreation and childcare together, this design would automatically produce an extended family feeling.

In this chapter I have made the point that no matter who
you are, there is probably a shared household to fit your
needs. There are many more types of these shared
households, or middle-class communes: While admit-

ting that his types overlap, Herbert Otto has described all of sixteen, including the nature commune (built around intensive gardening), the craft commune (organized for craft production), the art commune (composed of painters, sculptors, poets, and so on), and the teaching commune (conducting training sessions or operating a school). One more type is the commune whose members are trying out new sexual lifestyles. I have saved this type for the next chapter, which discusses closeness and sex.

3. COMMUNITY AND PRIVACY

People who get excited about living communally are usually torn two ways. They want the warmth and closeness of living with others, but they have fears about what it would mean. Some people are afraid that they might have to talk to housemates constantly, or that they might lose all privacy. Others fear that they might not find enough closeness in a communal household or just the reverse: There might be an expectation of more closeness or openness than they want. Couples may be concerned about how living communally will affect their relationship. Parents may be worried about losing control over their children in a household where other adults are present. Finally, some people worry that commune members might have sexual expectations that differ from their own. The idea behind this chapter is that an explanation of what actually happens in communes is helpful in dealing with these concerns about closeness and sex.

TOGETHERNESS

I have a friend who is greatly intrigued by communal living but imagines that it wouldn't work for her. "With all those people around," she worries, "I would have to talk to them all the time. I could never sit down and read the newspaper quietly." Many people share this worry: If people have chosen to live together so that they can "get close," they will work at it constantly. Perhaps after a week or two everyone will collapse from exhaustion.

Occasionally when a household has just formed, this comical situation actually happens. The members of one group followed one another from room to room during their first week of living together, on the assumption that such togetherness was expected. Then it dawned on them that they all wanted to spend some time alone.

In another new commune the members assumed that they were obligated to spend time with one another's guests. Since everyone had a lot of friends and relatives and the Thanksgiving and Christmas holiday season was in full swing, the group became trapped in a nonstop round of entertaining. It wasn't until after New Year that the flash of insight came: Why should everyone have to play host to other members' guests? With great relief it was agreed that people who didn't want to entertain could be elsewhere in the house and not feel guilty about it. Excessive togetherness is, at worst, only a temporary problem. There may be awkwardness in the very beginning, but when people realize that there is a problem they are able to strike a comfortable balance between time spent in company and time spent alone.

HOW CLOSE DO WE GET?

Most people agree on what togetherness is but have different notions of what it means to get close. Some people want companionship that, as months and years pass, may or may not ripen into close friendship. Others want close friendship from the start. To achieve this, they try to share their most personal feelings with their housemates, and they hope that their housemates will reciprocate in kind. People who want only companionship may find themselves in conflict with people who want close friendship and intimate sharing. This difficulty can be averted by living with people who want roughly the same level of closeness that you want.

The first commune I lived in is an example of a group where there was plenty of companionship, a sense of belonging, but little intimate sharing with the group as a whole. Nearly all members of this household were single and wanted to become involved with members of the opposite sex. Our romantic struggles, however, were too personal to become a topic of general conversation. Instead, when two members became fascinated with a method for beating the system at blackjack, discussion of their exploits at Lake Tahoe dominated the dinner conversation. Later, two other members enrolled in a human sexuality course and the conversation switched from gambling to sex—but stayed on an academic level because members did not discuss their own sex lives.

Companionship in this group sometimes meant evening excursions to the ice cream parlor or to a movie, but companionship was most readily available at home. With eight people in the house there was almost always someone in the kitchen or living room who felt like talking, and with many different interests represented there was always something to talk about. When we sat down to dinner together, our group resembled an old-fashioned family. In other respects we were more like a community where some members are closer than others. Two of the women became best friends. A man became a new member and after a few weeks he and a woman who had been a member for several years became a couple. A year and a half later they married.

David Wallechinsky, coauthor of *The People's Almanac*, lived in a group where there was more intense closeness and expects to write a novel about it some day. "We discussed not only our intellectual and political interests, but also what was going on in our emotional lives, the pains and sorrows and the good things too," Wallechinsky recalls. "At that time none of us had a stable love life, and we were all exploring and going through traumas and crises. We all went outside the house for our love relationships." Within the commune, these romantic crises were the constant topic of discussion. "We used each other to satisfy a lot of needs for companionship and emotional support and I really gained a lot from that."

The shared household made up of single young adults who build intense closeness by spending long hours discussing their romantic struggles is common. This is an exciting way to live, but it doesn't last forever. Members of the group eventually tend to find the stable love relationships they have been struggling toward. When this happens, the members have less personal information to share and they become less close.

Closeness and Privacy

In a classic work of sociology called *The Pursuit of Loneliness*, Philip Slater argues that Americans have been too successful in their search for privacy. "We seek more and more privacy," he says, "and feel more and more alienated and lonely when we get it." Many people don't understand that by single-mindedly pursuing the goal of a home in the suburbs, for example, they may cut themselves off from contact with other people. Because privacy is so popular, it is natural for people contemplating communal living to worry about it. Sociologist Rosabeth Kanter studied various aspects of life in middle-class communes, including privacy. She writes:

> Many members of contemporary communes have reported in interviews that they did give up some of their privacy when they joined the communes. However, they also assert either that they did not miss it, that they do not need as much privacy as they had thought, that they have learned to live without it, or most significantly, that the rewards they find in intimacy and closeness far outweigh the cost in privacy.

How can it be that people don't miss their privacy or don't need as much as they had thought? One reason is that commune members quickly recognize everyone's right to be alone, as I pointed out in the beginning of this chapter. Since most households have a policy of assigning a private bedroom to every member, being alone is easy. Close the door to your room and that's a signal that you don't want to be disturbed. Sometimes a group with children makes an exception to this policy and two kids share a room. And in some households couples share a room. But many people who live communally believe that both members of a couple should have their own room. This allows the partners to have privacy from each other.

Noise and Privacy

Unfortunately, a closed door may not prevent noise from entering and this can be bothersome if there are unruly children in the house or if your room is next to the kitchen, so that you hear pots and pans banging. Noise problems are eliminated, or at least greatly reduced, if you pick an older house with the thick walls that modern construction lacks (see Appendix B). But the most reliable protection against noise is simply the ability to ask for quiet—a skill discussed in the following chapter under the heading of "assertiveness."

Dealing With Depression

One of my former housemates was only twenty-two years old and lived with her parents before joining our commune. Periodically she felt depressed, and during these periods of depression she felt a lack of privacy. "My parents know how to treat me when I feel like this—you don't!" she explained unhappily. Some people have a habit of withdrawing from the world until their depression is over and they feel good about themselves once again. In a communal household, this kind of withdrawal isn't practical. Members must face each other at meals and in house meetings. Therefore, people who are accustomed to withdrawing when they are depressed do feel that there is not enough privacy.

Another housemate became depressed after she had

been searching for a job in her professional field without success. Each evening at dinner she would give us a colorful account of her job interview that day, including all the questions she had flubbed. By the end of dinner she would be restored to her usual happy self. She knew that hiding from others when she felt bad wasn't necessary; that in fact, sharing troubles with friends is a good way to feel better. Some people who have a habit of withdrawing when their self-esteem sags eventually make this liberating discovery. They are then able to live communally without feeling a lack of privacy.

Kanter's final point is that the rewards commune members find in intimacy and closeness more than make up for any loss in privacy. One commune member who works at home told me, "If I lived by myself it would be just my own phone calls, but when you live with five people and you're home by yourself, you become a telephone answering service." She found that mildly annoying, but added: "Having these people around totally outweighs any of the problems. I can depend on them and know that they really care about me and are always going to be there to cheer me on if I'm down in the dumps."

COUPLES IN COMMUNAL HOUSEHOLDS

A few years ago the word "couple" meant "married couple." Today the number of unmarried couples has greatly increased. As used in this book, "couple" means both the married and the unmarried pair. There is evidence that when a couple has a good relationship to begin with and chooses to live communally, the relationship can improve. The partners are likely to become at once more independent and more intimate. They may be able to recognize and abandon destructive habits that, over the years, can destroy a marriage.

To live successfully in a group, a couple must balance the time devoted to one another and the time given to

other members of the household. Some couples disap-
point housemates by avoiding contact with other members. Some other couples break up while living communally, usually because of strains present in their relationship before they decided to join a commune.

Independence in Commune Couples

Rosabeth Kanter's research team studied twenty-nine
couples living in communal households in Boston and
New Haven, Connecticut. Most of these couples were
married, and most told the researchers that before living
communally they had been treated "as an inseparable
twosome." They "rarely went places or maintained
friends alone, the wife was expected to identify and gain
status not from her own but from her husband's
achievements, and the two were taken as a single con-
versational unit, in which the opinion of one was assumed to stand for both." Being an inseparable twosome
is hard work. Often each partner feels uncomfortably
dependent on the other. One woman described her pre-
communal life with her husband like this: "I would nag
him for not spending time with me, and he would be
upset if I spent too many evenings at play rehearsal. With
no one else around we needed each other all the time."

When they began to live communally, these partners
became more independent. It was no longer necessary to
do everything together. One could go out, secure in the
knowledge that the other would not be left home alone.
There was someone else to talk to when a partner was
busy. It was possible to pursue an interest or a project
independent of the other. Although both partners liked
this new freedom, it was the women who had the most to
gain. For the first time they had a chance to develop their
own identities. My own interviews with couples who
live communally led to similar conclusions. "Society says
that when you get married the other person is supposed
to meet all of your needs," one wife told me. "But life
doesn't work that way, so women complain that 'my

husband never takes me anywhere.' Well, when you live in a commune there are other people you can do things with." One husband said, "When my wife goes out of town for a weekend workshop, I don't have to feel left out or alone, because there are other people around."

The researchers found that couples became more intimate when they no longer had to work at being inseparable and when the women developed their own identities and felt more equal to their mates. Dennis Jaffe describes the change like this: "As each person feels free to pursue his or her interests, separateness, and outside friendships, the power in the relationship becomes more equal, and each person sees the other on the basis of respect and acceptance of individuality, which in turn leads to greater openness and intimacy." One man explained how his relationship had changed in these words: "We've grown closer and talk about our feelings more. Our basic needs for independence, our unshared interests, get met in the house, which allows us to come together on the basis of real mutual concerns." A wife who lives communally told me, "Because my husband does some things on his own now, he has become a more interesting person and I can love him more."

Breaking Destructive Habits

Other researchers who have studied how communal living affects couples believe that it is a good antidote for the petty habits that married couples often torment each other with. Many of us have among our acquaintances a spouse who won't listen, withdraws from conflict, acts childishly, or nags. Over the years, this behavior can gradually destroy a marriage. "Living in a group teaches you to break destructive patterns," a wife reports. "You can't go on needling each other or picking on each other in a house where people are so actively trying to communicate—the petty squabbles seem so silly."

David and Eva Bradford believe that a commune is an excellent place for a couple to have destructive habits pointed out. The Bradfords note that housemates who offer this information must be caring and supportive and that the couple must not feel that their private life is being intruded upon. When these requirements are met, it is entirely possible to give and receive this kind of advice. Once when Jean and I were fighting I yelled at her in the insulting tone of voice that husbands use to cut wives down to size. A housemate recognized this tone from her married days and pointed it out to me. Since then I have yelled at Jean, but never in that tone of voice.

Maintaining Couple Intimacy

Couples who live communally face a challenge similar to that faced by couples who live in a close-knit community and must decide how much time to spend alone. If a couple spends too much time with housemates, the intimacy of their separate relationship may suffer. If the couple spends too little time with housemates, the others will be deprived of companionship and will resent it.

For most couples who live communally, striking a balance between time spent alone together and time spent with housemates is not terribly difficult. There are three ways that couples maintain the intimacy of their relationship while living communally: They stay in touch with their need to be alone together, they understand that total openness can endanger intimacy, and they are careful not to run away from fights with each other. Jean and I eat dinner with the whole group Monday through Friday. To nurture our separate relationship, we usually spend part of every evening and part of the weekend alone together. Other couples may discover that they need to spend less time or more time together. The goal is to be aware of how much time you need away from the others and to make sure this need is met.

Jean and I believe that being open with others is highly desirable, especially in communal living. But there are a few private aspects of our couple relationship that we don't discuss with others. Not sharing all seems to be a necessary part of intimacy. Couples who live communally need to be in agreement about which matters they choose not to share. Telling housemates information that your partner considers private is a good way to undermine your couple relationship, or at least to start a nasty fight.

Couples who don't like to fight may assume that living communally will deliver them from the necessity of fighting. A couple who lives alone has a great incentive to work through fights: When they aren't on speaking terms, there is no one else to talk to. When you live communally, there are others to talk to. Each partner can spend time with housemates while waiting for the fight to blow over. But this is a trap, since couples who avoid their conflicts tend to drift apart. Rosabeth Kanter found that this actually happened to some couples. Couples who live communally and wish to stay together may need to make a conscious effort to work through their conflicts rather than avoiding them by spending time with housemates.

Housemates can help a couple by not taking sides in a fight. In one household Kanter studied, other people took sides when a couple fought and this pushed the couple further apart. On the other hand, housemates can make themselves available as "therapeutic listeners" when one partner needs someone else to talk to. Listening without taking sides or making judgments can help a couple end their fight.

Couples Who Withdraw

Sometimes couples start eating alone together every night and avoiding contact with housemates in other ways. This behavior is unwelcome, as I mentioned, because other members feel left out. Often pairs who withdraw are newly formed and enjoying a highly romantic stage of their relationship. "All of their time and energy goes to each other and nothing goes to other people," one commune member said of such a couple. After a while, couples who have just come together usually get over their need to spend every moment with each other. A couple who persists in staying apart from the group is not being fair to the others. Such a couple really wants to live separately — and usually is encouraged to move out.

Sometimes when a couple withdraws it is not entirely the couple's fault. The tendency to withdraw has been unwittingly reinforced by housemates who are accustomed to treating any couple as a single unit rather than as two people. Communal living helps to alter this traditional perception of couples. Rooms, chores, and membership itself normally belong to individuals, not to couples. This makes it easier to see a couple as two people who have individual opinions and feelings as well as a special relationship with each other. When individuals who are coupled are seen and treated as individuals, the group is less likely to be faced with the problems of a withdrawing couple.

Couples Who Come Apart

Not all couples have a strong, healthy relationship when they begin to live communally. Some couples in Kanter's study believed that their marriages had broken down. Instead of separating they decided to try living communally. These last-ditch efforts to save a relationship failed and the couples separated. The study indicated that couples are likely to separate while living communally if their relationship is already badly strained in one of the following ways:

> They have an "empty-shell" marriage
> They have conflicting reasons for wanting to live com-
> munally
> They are strongly influenced by "anti-couple" beliefs

Kanter defined an "empty-shell" marriage as one that is no longer held together by affection, admiration, or love. Instead, the couple is bound together by the legal institution of marriage and by mutual insecurity. Each

partner thinks, "I must stay in this relationship no matter
how unpleasant it gets, because my spouse is the only
person who will stand by me." Living communally, an
empty-shell couple discovers that housemates can provide companionship and emotional support. Remaining
trapped with each other is no longer necessary, so they
separate.

The conflicting reasons for wanting to live communally mostly involved sex or sex roles. One husband who
felt trapped in marriage fantasized that the commune
would provide him with additional sex partners, but his
wife had no intention of abandoning sexual monogamy.
Her reasons for living communally were to escape her
isolated existence in the suburbs and to achieve a
stronger sense of her own identity. This couple broke up
when the husband had an affair. Another wife expected
that her husband would care for their children when they
lived communally, freeing her to return to school. When
he did not stay home to care for the kids, she left him.

Nearly all of the couples who broke up held radical
feminist beliefs and lived with housemates who reinforced these beliefs. "Feminist values induced some
women to deliberately seek communalism and sacrifice
their marriages," the researchers wrote. "The women
mentioned that they wanted to live communally because
they felt they could get certain kinds of emotional support only from other women; some said they wanted to
identify with their own sex rather than with their husband and couple." Most couples who live communally
hold some feminist beliefs. They feel, for example, that
men should do an equal share of the housework. But few
couples who live communally subscribe to the anti-
nuclear-family ideology that some of the Boston and
New Haven couples held.

What does all this mean to a couple that is contemplating living communally? Such a couple might have a
heart-to-heart talk, revealing to each other their reasons
for wanting to live communally. If they detect serious

strains or incompatible motives, they could work on strengthening their relationship before deciding to live communally.

CHILDREN: NO LONGER
THE PARENT'S "PROPERTY"

Like their parents, children tend to grow less dependent, develop individual identities, and get closer to other people when they live communally. Communal living runs counter to the tendency to view a child merely as an extension of the parent's personality or, worse yet, as the parent's "property." Kanter's research team found that two changes occur when parents live communally with their kids:

1. Parents are no longer the only people making rules for their children. Parents share some of their authority with other commune members. An example is when the adults get together and decide — with some participation from the kids — what kids will eat or when they will be allowed to watch TV.

2. Parents are less able to act as mediators between their child and other people. In a commune parents can't oversee all aspects of a child's daily life with other members. Children form their own relationships with the other adults and kids in the group.

No longer dependent on their parents to make rules or to decide how they will relate to others, children see themselves more as individuals. Parents, too, begin to see kids this way. Sometimes parents resist this change, believing that they are losing too much control over their children. But most parents who live communally believe that it is a good way for children to gradually let go of apron strings and grow more independent.

Susan Dun, a family therapist who has observed many communal households, believes that the presence of other adult figures is healthy for parents. When parents are the only adults in their child's world, they feel totally responsible for the child's problems and for the way the child will eventually turn out as an adult, Dun explains. Many parents worry constantly whether they are doing the right thing, and their anxiety is transmitted to their children. Parents who no longer see themselves as the only ones shaping their child's development can relax, enjoy their kids, and give them more affection and support.

Finding People Who Enjoy Children

Adding other adults to a child's world isn't always as easy as parents hope it will be. The problem is that many adults in our society have little interest in children and don't want to spend time with them. So it is necessary to select the other adults carefully, choosing people who genuinely like kids. One father who lives communally with his two small children told me, "Everybody likes kids, you know. In the abstract." He discovered that it isn't enough to ask casually how a prospective household member feels about kids. To get a useful answer, it helps to probe a little—to find out how much prospective members know about kids, whether they have ever lived with kids in the past, and so on. Fortunately, there are people who truly love children and really want to live with them, even though they have none of their own. Dennis Jaffe explains what attracts such people to communal living: "Nonparents have an opportunity to live with children, learn about them, without having to have major responsibility for them or for a family. They are like bachelor aunts or uncles who are important parts of the family and play important roles for the children." These are the kinds of people parents want to join their communal households.

Including Children in the Life of the Group

Sometimes parents are only partially successful, and their children become part of a household where the nonparents don't understand kids very well or don't bother to include kids in many activities. Some communes manage to remedy this. In West Philadelphia, nonviolent political activists live in twenty communal households that make up the Philadelphia Life Center. When single parents and their children first moved into these households, many of the nonparents viewed the kids as a burden and didn't want to help with childrearing. The parents protested that children should be an important part of the households. After some debate everyone agreed that the nonparents needed to learn more about children, and the entire adult membership of several households took a Parent Effectiveness Training course. This was the beginning of a new and more positive attitude toward children in these households. P.E.T. emphasizes clear two-way communication between adults and children, provides a method of resolving conflicts between adults and children, and helps families — or communes — to enjoy warmer feelings and closer relationships. In addition to the training course, there is also a book entitled *P.E.T.: Parent Effectiveness Training* by Dr. Thomas Gordon.

Some communal households have deliberately designed projects to include children more fully in the daily life of the group. Says psychologist Judith Blanton, who has lived communally with children: "You can build a play area together, write a story together, or put on a play together. Activities like these are fun for adults and kids alike, and they are one way to unify a communal household." Special projects are only one way to include kids in the life of the group. Children can also be included in house meetings (see Chapter Five) and in communal housekeeping (see Chapter Six).

SEX

Even people who aren't interested in living communally want to know about sexual practices in shared households. I tell them that it depends on the household and its members. Many couples who live communally are sexually monogamous. Single people who live communally tend to have romantic partners who live outside the group. But sometimes two single members who belong to the same commune become romantically involved with each other. A few middle-class communes are sexually experimental—the members are searching beyond monogamy for greater sexual freedom.

In family households there is often a clear understanding that everyone intends to remain monogamous. A member of a Boston commune that has six adults (mostly single parents) and five children says, "One of our goals is stability." If the adults had affairs with one another, a member who felt left out could become jealous. Or a pair might start an affair only to break it off. In either case, someone who felt rejected sexually might leave the group. This kind of instability is what the members hope to avoid by not having sexual relationships with each other.

Dealing With Sexual Attractions

People who don't live communally sometimes feel attracted to a friend or acquaintance. When this happens they have a choice: They can act on the sexual attraction, or they can continue to have sexual relations only with their partner. The same choice presents itself to couples who live communally. Sometimes a commune member feels attracted to another member. Usually the choice is not to act on the attraction and it doesn't cause any problem. When a sexual attraction does lead to strained feelings, David Bradford believes that open communication is the best solution. "By discussing the attraction openly," he says, "couples are sometimes able to accept the attraction but have less need to act on it. What seems to be the most destructive is not to deal directly with it, for that only produces tension."

Some writers contend that commune members are like brothers and sisters who wouldn't dream of having sex with one another. Such an "incest taboo" may actually exist in Israeli communes. A study of 2,769 Israeli weddings showed that not one had taken place between two adults who had lived together on a kibbutz as children. In many communal households in this country, male and female members do treat each other as siblings. There is hugging and other affectionate touching without erotic overtones. Single people need this kind of warmth and affection, and living communally is a good way to get it. But there isn't any universal incest taboo in American communes, since single members do sometimes become sexually involved.

Having an Affair With a Housemate

Two members who become sexually involved often become a couple. As I mentioned earlier in this chapter, I lived with one couple who met when the male partner joined the commune. Eventually they married. Other couples who meet in this way may break up after a year or two. When this happens, continuing to live together is usually painful, and one or both persons leaves the commune.

Although it is possible to become coupled with another household member, it is very difficult to have a "casual affair" with another member. Most people who live communally are fully aware that casual affairs work better when you don't live with the other person. That way you simply stop seeing each other when one or both persons tire of the affair. In a commune you can't stop seeing the other person, and this can cause serious complications. I know a handful of people who have been able to enjoy brief affairs with a housemate, end the sexual relationship on a pleasant note, and continue to live together as friends. Most people have trouble doing this. One or even both of them feel rejected and angry when the affair ends, and one or both may find it necessary to move out.

Nonmonogamous Households

People who have a high tolerance for emotional ups and downs and a low tolerance for monogamy have established communal households where some form of sexual freedom is the goal. A group marriage is a commune, usually formed by married couples, in which there is an expectation that the adults will become sexually involved with all other members of the opposite sex. Novelist Robert Rimmer has written several books on this theme. But group marriages are easier to achieve in theory than in reality. Family Synergy, an organization of people interested in sexually open relationships, reports that the median duration of actual group marriages is only sixteen months. To anyone who wants to learn more about this subject, I recommend the carefully written book *Group Marriage* by Larry and Joan Constantine.

Some other communes promote alternatives to monogamy without seeking to become group marriages. Members of Bayland House in Campbell, California, encourage one another in their efforts to maintain more than one sexual relationship, either with other members or with outsiders. In the winter of 1978 the group had eight members ranging in age from twenty-four to forty-five, and half of them had a relationship inside the house. Three members had been part of the group for over five years, two had been there for three years, two more had been there two years, and two members had just moved out. One member had only one relationship, but everyone else had more than one. The members of this commune have succeeded in having multiple relationships, although the pairs often change and the membership of the house itself has not stabilized.

A few years ago there was greater enthusiasm in commune circles for group marriages, "open" relationships, and similar experiments. Today some of this enthusiasm has cooled, partly because people who thought they were capable of having "nonpossessive, nonexclusive" relationships discovered that this wasn't what they wanted after all. The problem is that a commune is a social experiment to begin with. When a group decides to experiment with new sexual patterns at the same time that it is learning how to live communally, it takes on two experiments at once. This greatly increases the risk of failure—especially since sex is, for most people, such an emotionally charged part of life.

There are more choices in communal living than appear possible at first. People who want intense personal sharing and closeness can find it by choosing the right households. Simple companionship and a sense of community, without intense sharing or closeness, are available in other groups. Privacy is less of a problem than people fear; commune members can close the door to their room and not have to worry about someone disturbing them. Couples manage to balance the time they devote to each other and the time they give to the group, and often couple relationships improve. Parents do lose some control over their kids, but this is usually seen as an advantage, not a problem. Finally, there are plenty of sexual choices in communes. Early in this chapter I noted that when members of the same commune have different expectations about closeness, conflict is the likely result. The next chapter suggests how to avoid this difficulty, and how to deal with other kinds of conflicts in communal life.

4. RESOLVING CONFLICT

When people rub shoulders often, they are bound to rub each other the wrong way part of the time. Conflict is part of life in nuclear families, neighborhoods, schools, businesses—and in communes. There is one way of dealing with conflict that doesn't work, either in traditional families or in communes: pretending that nothing is wrong. Sooner or later the conflict usually surfaces in exaggerated form.

People who live communally realize that some conflict is inevitable but try to keep it to a minimum. People who are founding a new commune compare their expectations carefully. This helps avert certain conflicts. Additional clashes are prevented at the founding stage by making a few agreements — most importantly, by agreeing in advance on how future members will be admitted to the household. The first part of this chapter is about preventing conflict when a new commune is being planned. The rest of the chapter explains how commune members cope with the everyday conflicts that are part of living together. People who live communally often discover that they can reconcile disagreements better by becoming more assertive. Everyday conflicts also become easier to resolve when members take responsibility for their own feelings. These interpersonal skills, which tend to develop naturally in communal living, are also described in popular books and can be practiced in workshops and small groups.

BEFORE YOU LIVE TOGETHER: PREVENTING CONFLICT

When the first middle-class communes were formed at the beginning of the 1970s, there were no successful models to follow. Inevitably the early groups made mistakes. Two common ones were made by twelve adults who came together in late 1969 in a university town in the Midwest. L. Dave Brown and his wife Jane were social scientists acting as consultants to this group. According to their account, the people who met to plan the commune made no attempt to develop a common expectation about which activities members would participate in when they were living together. The group also failed to reach agreement on how new members would be admitted.

The impact of these oversights became apparent after the members had purchased a three-story house and moved in. The group's two married couples had three small children, bringing the total membership to fifteen and filling the house to capacity or beyond, depending on how you define overcrowding. But within the first year three single men became engaged and invited their fiancées to join them in the commune. Prior agreement on a procedure for admitting new members would have prevented the conflict that followed. The members who considered the house to be filled to capacity opposed taking in more people, while the engaged men and their supporters contended that members had a right to bring a future spouse into the group. The three women moved in but the dispute continued.

Meanwhile, the group was being divided in another way. Some members believed that the purpose of living communally was to enable people to do as many things as possible together. They wanted the whole group to go to political rallies, take weekend trips to the mountains, help to rebuild the house, and attend a workshop led by the Browns. Other members were less committed to togetherness. True, they had helped remodel the house, they liked eating dinner with the others, and they enjoyed late-night socializing in the kitchen. But they had little interest in organized outings or other outside activities involving the whole group. Disagreement between the advocates of more or fewer shared activities continued for over a year. Eventually most of the members who wanted less togetherness moved out.

Such problems can be avoided by discussing members' expectations openly before the commune is formed and by agreeing on guidelines for resolution of future conflicts.

Comparing Expectations

Today it is standard practice for people to share their expectations about what members will do together when a commune is in the planning stages. If a serious conflict arises, changes can be made before people actually move in together. For example, there could be a decision to start two households—one for the people who want much togetherness, and another for the people who want to live more independently. It is wise to compare expectations concerning other aspects of communal life as well. Questions that can be discussed ahead of time are mentioned throughout this book and are summed up in a checklist that appears in Chapter Seven.

Advance Agreements

The time to make an agreement covering admission of new members is before you move into a communal home. You could wait, as the Midwest group did, until someone wants your commune to admit a fiancé, a lover, or a child who has been in the custody of the other parent

—but that is asking for trouble. A group can tailor an admissions policy to meet its own needs, but one policy is shared by all the communes I have ever seen: A new person can join only with the unanimous agreement of all members. This means that any member who is opposed to living with a candidate for membership can exercise a veto and prevent the candidate's admission. This veto system has advantages and disadvantages, which are discussed in Chapter Eight. Most groups also agree on the number of people who will live in the house. Over the years this number may increase or decrease, but only by unanimous agreement. Agreements that groups may want to make in advance are also summarized in the Chapter Seven checklist.

DEALING WITH DAY-TO-DAY CONFLICTS

Asking the right questions and making a few agreements when a commune is in the planning stages will produce a more harmonious household. But there is no way to avert the day-to-day conflicts that are always part of living with others, whether you live communally or in a nuclear family. Fortunately these conflicts are no reason for despair; they have a silver lining. Thomas Gordon, author of *Parent Effectiveness Training*, puts it this way: "Conflicts can push people away from each other or pull them into a closer and more intimate union; they contain the seeds of destruction and the seeds of greater unity; they may bring about armed warfare or deeper mutual understanding."

To show how the apparent paradox in this statement can be resolved, let's take an example. In a newly formed household, Richard played his stereo at full volume. Lynn was bothered by the music but afraid to say anything about it. The conflict clearly was pushing the two members apart. When Lynn found the courage to speak up, Richard listened understandingly, and they experimented with volume settings until they found one that kept the music in his room. The two housemates also agreed that when Lynn left the house, she would let him know so that he could play the music more loudly. In the course of resolving this conflict, they learned that they cared enough about each other to be genuinely interested in their problems, and both were willing to compromise to resolve the conflict. The process brought them closer together than they had been before. That's the silver lining.

Being Assertive

Like Lynn did at first, people who live communally are often tempted to deal with conflict by keeping quiet and hoping to avoid it. Soon they discover that although avoiding conflict doesn't work, becoming more assertive does work. To prevent any misunderstanding, I should define what I mean by being "assertive." I don't mean being aggressive or intimidating. Being assertive is speaking up when something is bothering you or when you want to ask for something. When assertive people ask for something, they don't demand; they respect the other person's right to say yes or no.

Many communal conflicts can be eliminated when the members become more assertive. The loud music problem has been resolved, so let's take another example. The most familiar communal complaint of all is a disagreement about housekeeping. Suppose I'm angry because the house isn't neat enough to suit me. If I'm unassertive I don't let the others know that I'm unhappy and propose improvements in our housekeeping system. My anger comes out another way. For example:

1. I become the house martyr. I do more cleaning than anyone else, and I exact a price for the work. I complain a lot and keep reminding everyone else that I'm doing more than my share. If I succeed completely they feel guilty. From time to time they may even be shamed into doing more housework, although this is far from certain.

2. I take note when other members make messes and

fail to clean them up, silently storing the memory of these offenses in my mental "gunnysack." When I have stored up enough, I get angry at these people. My anger may intimidate someone into being neater for a few days. But then the cycle repeats itself. I again gunnysack my complaints until I feel entitled to another burst of anger.

3. Instead of becoming actively aggressive, as in the previous example, I become passively aggressive. I "forget" to do my chores or I "forget" to write down the telephone messages I have taken for other house members. I may even "forget" to make dinner, or I may "accidentally" break dishes and burn pots and pans.

4. I become moody and rarely have much to say. Perhaps I spend most of my time in my room. After a while I may get bored with withdrawing partially from the others in this way. So I accomplish the ultimate withdrawal: I move out.

Compared with these four alternatives, assertiveness is the best path to take. Just like members of a nuclear family, members of a shared household choose how they try to influence one another. They can be assertive and ask directly for what they want. Or they can seek to manipulate one another with guilt, intimidation, or emotional or physical withdrawal.

It is not always necessary to behave assertively in communal living, however. In some situations, commune members don't have to ask for anything—they can resolve conflicts within themselves by taking responsibility for their own feelings.

Taking Responsibility

The easiest way to explain this method of handling conflict is to give you examples again. Several years ago, when I joined Napa House, there were often crumbs on our kitchen counter. Being a new member and wanting to make a good impression, I dutifully swept them away when it was my turn to tidy up the kitchen. I soon noticed that when other members had kitchen duty, sometimes the crumbs weren't cleaned up. I began to feel self-righteously resentful about this. Then I remembered that I had visited Napa House several times before joining. On some of those occasions there were crumbs scattered around the kitchen counter. When I decided to join, I knew the standard of cleanliness for the kitchen was different from my personal standard. Therefore, I had no reason to feel resentful or self-righteous about the crumbs. I could speak up about them and try to persuade the others to adopt my standard or I could accept matters the way they stood. I tried accepting crumbs left by others and becoming a less compulsive crumb sweeper myself. My resentment vanished.

Here's another example from my early days at Napa House. I hadn't met my wife Jean then. I didn't even have a romantic relationship. But one of our housemates —I'll call him Francisco—had several woman friends. One of them was a dinner guest several nights a week, although neither she nor Francisco contributed anything to our food kitty to pay for her meals. This bothered me. I was planning to raise the question in the next house meeting when I realized that I wasn't just bothered — I was furious, and there was no rational basis for such anger. Then the insight hit: My anger had little to do with the food kitty and much to do with my being envious of Francisco because he had girl friends. As soon as I became aware that I was envious, I realized that I didn't have to compare myself with Francisco. My envy and anger vanished, leaving only mild concern over our finances. I raised the question at our next meeting and we agreed without difficulty that regular guests would contribute to the food kitty.

My experiences with crumbs and envy illustrate how commune members can resolve a conflict by taking responsibility for examining their own feelings. Taking responsibility is extremely effective when it works. Unfortunately, it doesn't work every time. Often resentment will persist until you talk to the member who is

annoying you. Communal living is much easier when
members have the ability both to be assertive and to take
responsibility and can call forth the appropriate ability
for a given situation. Living communally perfects both of
these skills. "I've learned to speak up if something
bothers me," says a member of a Massachusetts commune. "But I've also become more tolerant."

I can't resist telling you the sequel to the crumbs story.
A year after I joined Napa House, several other members
decided they wanted to live with fewer crumbs. We all
agreed to this and now there is rarely a crumb in sight.
The change has been easy for me—I've simply reverted
to my old standard, becoming once again a zealous
crumb hunter. Living communally, people discover
either that they are more adaptable than they thought or
that they can learn to be.

How to Improve Interpersonal Skills

Interpersonal skills such as assertiveness and taking responsibility for feelings are useful in communal living, if
not essential. Some commune members find these skills
so helpful that they aren't content just to practice them in
everyday living. They take workshops or read books on
the subject. There are thousands of workshops, small
group experiences, and books that explore this area.
Some groups teach the basic communication skills;
others go more deeply into the development of self-
awareness and relationships and can be more threatening to people's beliefs and assumptions about themselves. What follows isn't a definitive guide by any
means. It's an attempt to outline some of the resources
that people who live communally have found useful.

Assertiveness training workshops. Assertiveness
training has been popular among women who want to
learn how to say what they want without being aggressive or intimidating. Now there are also assertiveness
workshops designed for both sexes. An assertiveness
workshop that focuses on personal relationships, rather
than on dealing with sales people in stores or on man-

aging people at work, is most relevant to communal living. Participants in these workshops are not pressured to reveal personal details of their lives. Nor do they attack one another. People who haven't participated in personal growth groups before can feel safe in this kind of workshop.

Communication workshops. How to listen to another person in a supportive and understanding way is the most important skill taught here. Listening skills are a big plus in communes, since housemates are hard to live with when they feel misunderstood. This is also a non-threatening workshop for people who haven't been in groups before — there is no pressure to disclose personal information, and participants don't attack one another. Instead the emphasis is on learning to understand and accept other people as they are.

Gestalt groups. This kind of group, which may be advertised as either a growth experience or group psychotherapy, presents an opportunity to learn about taking responsibility. Participants deal with inner conflicts, with the goal of clarifying how they feel and what they want. This is important to communal living, since the more self-aware you become, the easier and the more fun it is to live with others who have different goals and desires. The aim in this group is for participants to deal with their own problems, not to challenge other members of the group. But they are expected to talk about their personal feelings, so the gestalt group is more threatening than an assertiveness training or communication workshop.

Encounter groups. These sessions are based on the expectation that participants will reveal exactly how they feel about one another. Members who try to cover up their feelings are likely to be attacked by other members. This is the most threatening kind of group, but for some people it is also the most fun and the most useful. When I joined Napa House, I had a habit of attempting to appear calm and agreeable when I was annoyed or angry. This irritated my housemates and they told me so. About the same time I happened to join an encounter group, and there I got the same negative reaction to my false front. I was forced to admit that my housemates might be right. I tried to notice when I was angry and to stop pretending to feel something else. The results were dramatic. I found that I could handle disagreements more effectively and with less anxiety and strain, and my housemates started liking me more.

These are only a few of the workshops and groups that deal with interpersonal relations. There are other kinds, some of which are quite useful in communal living. But that's something you can decide for yourself when you learn which groups are available in your community. One word of caution applies to all of these groups and workshops. Some of the leaders are excellent, while others do not have the ability necessary for guiding such a group. An academic degree doesn't guarantee that you will be in competent hands — some of the most effective leaders don't have a degree, and some of the incompetent people do. To make sure that you're not wasting your money, find people who know about a group and its leader and ask their opinion.

Books on interpersonal skills. Books are usually easy to evaluate — often the cover alone identifies a gimmicky, unhelpful approach. Anything with the word "intimidation" on the cover is worse than useless in communal living. The last thing housemates want is for you to intimidate them, to "look out for number one," or to use any of the other alienating techniques that some authors are selling. Fortunately, the popular psychology explosion has also produced sound and practical volumes. The best way to select one of these is to go to a bookstore or a library and examine the books yourself or to ask someone whose opinion you respect. I will mention only five books here. Many bookstores stock an entire shelf with paperback books about assertiveness. Two that I like are *Don't Say Yes When You Want to Say No* by Herbert Fensterheim and *When I Say No, I Feel Guilty* by Manuel Smith. *Parent Effectiveness Training* has already been mentioned; it is an excellent guide to clear, caring communication not only with children, but with anyone, and it explains a method of resolving conflicts that some communal households may want to try. Many books explain the concept of taking responsibility for feelings. Two good ones are *Be the Person You Were Meant To Be* by Jerry Greenwald and *Your Erroneous Zones* by Wayne Dyer.

This chapter has explored three ways to deal with conflict in communal living. First, expectations can be compared at the planning stage. If extreme differences are detected, people can leave or enter the planning group so that those who finally live together have compatible expectations. Second, additional conflicts can be prevented by making certain agreements, a few of which need to be reached before the group moves into its house. Third, once people are living together members can handle everyday frictions with far greater ease if they are assertive and if they are careful to be aware of their own feelings.

There is a fourth way of dealing with conflict that is just as important as the first three. Members can make sure decisions are made in a fair way that prevents or resolves conflict. They can provide a forum — the house meeting — where members who are unhappy about any aspect of communal life can be heard and where solutions to the group's problems can be found. Most minor decisions are not made in a house meeting, however. When members also pay attention to how informal decisions are made outside the house meeting, they gain another means to promote harmony and warm, familylike feelings. The subject of the next chapter is communal decision making.

5. COMMUNITY DECISION MAKING

A market survey person telephoned the other day and wanted to talk to the "male head" of our household. She said goodbye quickly when I told her, "This is a commune, so we don't have any head of the household, male or female." I suspect this was an unsettling experience for her. "Without a male head of the household," she must still be wondering, "how do they decide what kind of lawn mower to buy?" This chapter will provide some answers to her question.

Like anybody else, people who live communally realize that life is full of big decisions and little decisions. In a commune, a big decision might be whether to paint the house, whom to choose as a new member, whether to increase the food budget to keep pace with inflation — or whether to buy a new lawn mower. The big decisions are usually made in a house meeting, which gives everyone a chance to voice an opinion.

Little decisions are legion. Maybe Joe wants to cook dinner late on Thursday because he's going to have to work overtime, Sue wants to make sure her friend from out of town can be a house guest next week, or Mike doesn't know what kind of floor wax to buy. These decisions can be made in a house meeting but are usually made informally. Decisions are made informally when a

member who wants to do something asks around to
make sure there are no objections or when a member
with special expertise is recognized as a leader at, for
example, gardening or keeping the house books. Unilateral decisions — those made by a member without consulting the others — often cause problems.

Nuclear families manage to struggle along without
house meetings. Meetings are necessary in shared
households, however, because they are run by consensus. All members, or at least all adult members, are equal
participants. The only way they can make big decisions is
for everyone to agree. If someone isn't around, a big
decision can't be made. So it's easier to say, "Okay, we'll
all get together at seven o'clock on Tuesday."

The necessity of deciding by consensus is one reason
that house meetings are a must. Another reason is emotional. Communes aren't held together by sex roles or
marriage vows as nuclear families are. Communes hold
together because the members care about each other and
want to be together. Somebody who is unhappy about
something in the commune needs to let the other members know, and needs to see evidence that they care. One
of the best ways to reassure one another that everyone
does care is to hold a house meeting and use it to air
people's complaints. When members come to a meeting
and listen to one another, that's tangible proof that they
care. Many gripes vanish as if by magic when the
member with the complaint airs it and is reassured that
the others are genuinely sympathetic. When this happens, the group doesn't have to take any action to resolve
the problem because it has solved itself.

Other complaints do require action. For example,
someone who violates the expectation that all members
will be equal or that everyone will share the housework
equally must be persuaded to behave differently. The
only power that the group has to confront an uncooperative or inconsiderate member is the moral suasion that
can be mustered in a house meeting. People who aren't
familiar with middle-class communes sometimes as-

sume that, as in the guru-led communes, the group exercises great power over its members. In reality, middle-class communes have no leader and are composed of members whose strongest values include equality and individualism. The tendency they must combat is for members to be extremely individualistic and to deny the group any legitimate power at all. The tendency is toward anarchy, not dictatorship. If this tendency were to go totally unchecked, cooperation would be impossible. The house meeting is needed to provide a counterbalance to extreme individualism and, on occasion, to serve as a forum where uncooperative members can be confronted and persuaded to be more considerate. House meetings are essential in protecting the rights of the group as a whole.

WHEN TO HAVE HOUSE MEETINGS

Some groups find that they don't need to hold a house meeting every week. "If people get the feeling that things are really going downhill, we call a house meeting," says a member of a close-knit household of six people. A few weeks or even a month or two can go by between meetings at his commune. All of the members have lived communally for several years, all are excellent communicators, and they seem to do just fine without a regularly scheduled meeting.

Other people who live communally insist that in their households "things go downhill" without fail unless they hold a meeting every week. New communes often find that regular meetings are necessary to arrange the details of running a household — to decide how to organize food buying and cooking, cleaning chores, childcare, and so forth. Larger groups, as I explained in Chapter Two, usually need to meet regularly to coordinate the activities of their many members and to keep their complex lines of communication open. Holding a weekly meeting has important advantages. Resentments intensify if members don't air them promptly. A regular meeting encourages members to talk about things that bother them.

Some groups agree that, although there will be no regularly scheduled meetings, a meeting will be held whenever a member requests it. This can work splendidly if you have a houseful of assertive people. In households where some members aren't assertive, this system breaks down. The unassertive members don't get around to calling a meeting while their resentments are still small. They wait until little annoyances have blossomed into an emotional crisis. Then they call a meeting.

MEETING STYLES

The communal house meeting is the commune's House and Senate and Presidency all wrapped into one. Visually, however, a house meeting does not appear so impressive. Usually, it is just a group of people sprawled around the living room or perhaps seated at the kitchen table sipping coffee. Some households meet successfully with no agenda and no chairperson, while other groups have a written agenda and a rotating chairperson. One popular way to set up the agenda is to post a blank sheet of paper in the kitchen and head it "Agenda." As members think of items they want to bring up in the meeting, they jot them down. This helps ensure that important matters aren't forgotten. Some groups go down their agenda in orderly fashion. In other households, meetings are frequently interrupted by lengthy digressions, laughter, and other enjoyable but unbusinesslike antics. The general rule is that people should get what they want. If some members don't feel that they are being heard, perhaps meetings need to become more orderly or less rushed. If meetings seem dry and boring, perhaps they need to be less businesslike so that it is easier for people to express feelings.

Attendance

No matter how informal their meetings may be, communal households stress the importance of having everyone attend. When there is an important decision to be made by consensus, no action can be taken if someone is absent. The matter must be held over until the next meeting. Or suppose that someone is angry about something that another member has done. There is little point in bringing this up in the meeting if the offender isn't there to hear the complaint.

Important as attendance is, groups cannot have rigid rules that say, "You will be here at the appointed hour, or else." Our household is fairly typical. Members of Napa House take care not to schedule conflicting activities for 5 P.M. Tuesday, our meeting time. But if there is an activity of unusual importance to a member, we make an exception. That week's meeting is shifted to another hour or another day. Groups find that the best way to encourage attendance is to state the expectation that people will come. This means that when a new household is being planned, the question of meetings has to be discussed. The group needs to decide whether a regular meeting will be held and to be sure that everyone is in agreement about the importance of attending meetings. Expectations concerning meetings also need to be stated clearly when a commune recruits new members.

Kids Can Take Part

In most communes, children attend house meetings on an equal basis with the adults. This reflects their parents' belief that full participation in the life of the household is a healthy learning experience for kids. Parents also know that kids are more likely to cooperate in carrying out decisions when they have had a share in making them. Sometimes a child feels that meetings are a grownup activity and doesn't want to attend. Claude Steiner believes the way to avoid this is to treat kids as equal members of the household who, in every possible way, have the same rights and responsibilities as the adults. Steiner explains that in his household our attitude is that children don't have as many skills as adults, but we treat them like grownups with whatever capacities they have. If the kids miss the meetings, we resent it, and they're given the same kind of treatment as the grownups: grownups who miss the meetings just because they are playing would catch hell, and so would the kids. If a grownup just sits there and doesn't say anything the whole meeting, somebody will probably say, "Look, I don't like you just sitting there, I would like you to say something." Kids are treated the same way. And when kids talk, we listen. We don't discount their contributions. We realize that what they say in meetings is a very important part of their becoming equal participants in the house.

Children who are treated as equal participants use house meetings to ask for what they want. In one commune, a ten-year-old spoke up to complain that an adult had been teasing him. The teasing stopped. In another household, a nine-year-old told a house meeting, "I'm the only child here, and it's a drag. You have plenty of adults to be with, and I don't have any children to be with." A few months later when someone moved out, the group chose a mother and ten-year-old child to move in.

Kids sometimes speak up to complain that they must contend with too many adult bosses and too many rules. Rosabeth Kanter believes that this complaint is often justified. In the communes that she studied, children encountered too many people saying, "Stop that." Sometimes one adult would enforce a rule and another adult would ignore it. Kids who participate in house meetings get a chance to set things right if they feel that adults are issuing too many orders or are enforcing rules inconsistently.

CREATING A FAVORABLE CLIMATE FOR CONSENSUS

Sometimes people disagree about whether the house needs painting, whether to buy only whole wheat bread because it's healthier, or whether a guest is welcome to stay longer. These and a thousand other decisions can't be made if the members can't reach a consensus. The key to reaching a consensus is this: People will disagree stubbornly when they don't feel that their views have been heard or respected. When members do feel understood and respected, it's much easier to reach a consensus. I remember a house meeting that bogged down for what seemed like hours over the seemingly trivial issue of whether to add English muffins to our communal shopping list. Two women were strongly opposed, not so much to the muffins as to the behavior of the male member who suggested buying them. They felt that he didn't listen to them and that their feelings didn't really count with him. So they wouldn't agree to buy the muffins he liked so much.

Some groups take deliberate steps to make sure that everyone's views are heard. The members sit in a circle, and when an emotionally charged issue is discussed, each person speaks in turn. To make sure that a member has finished, the next person allows a few seconds of silence to elapse before talking. It is possible to cultivate good communication habits without adopting this meeting format if members don't interrupt and if they make sure everyone has a chance to speak.

No-Lose Problem Solving

If a climate has been created in which everyone feels respected—and you respectfully disagree—you can use the house meeting to search for a creative solution that hadn't occurred to anyone and that everyone can embrace enthusiastically. The following story shows how one group did this.

Communes, like nuclear families, are sometimes visited by guests who overstay their welcome. Jack, a member of an Oakland, California, commune invited two friends to stay at the house when they were in town. They stayed a week and left. After a few days, they reappeared and stayed another week. The third time they came, members began to feel uncomfortable. There had never been an indication of how long these guests would stay. The problem was brought up in the house meeting, and no one had a solution. Several members insisted that Jack had the responsibility to tell his guests how long they could stay. Jack admitted that he didn't have the courage to do this. The stalemate was broken when one of the members offered a new idea: They could adopt a house policy regulating how long guests can stay. This solution pleased everyone. Jack liked it because, backed by official house policy, he would be able to say no to his guests at last. The others liked it because from then on they would be protected against guests overstaying their welcome.

Sometimes it isn't possible to find a solution that pleases everyone, and the group has to settle for a compromise solution. When members meet each other halfway in a compromise, chances are that no one will be completely satisfied. All members may feel that they have lost something. The guest policy example shows that it is possible to reach a solution that is better than a compromise: The Oakland group came up with a creative solution that made everybody a winner. Thomas Gordon calls this "no-lose problem solving." The method is described step-by-step in his book *Parent Effectiveness Training*.

DECIDING INFORMALLY

As I said at the beginning of this chapter, little decisions are sometimes made in a house meeting, but more often they are made informally. So many little decisions need to be made that making all of them in a house meeting would take far too long. Occasionally, though, commune members do put themselves into this fix, especially if their group is new.

Dennis Jaffe observed what happened in a commune where it was believed that the smallest issues had to be settled in a meeting. The members, he reports, "felt frustrated and powerless because a lone dissenter could block a decision, and endless hours were spent on minor details." Eventually a way around this impasse was found:

> As people became more trusting of each other and more in general agreement as to how things should be done, people began to take the initiative to do things on their own. Currently, if one wants to do something, like build a bicycle shed, have a party or rearrange a room, a person asks around to see if there are objections, and if there are none, simply acts.

Asking around is a much-used way of making small decisions. If the project will affect others, the person who asks around assumes an obligation to check with everybody. Hearing no objection, the asker is authorized to proceed.

A Houseful of Leaders

Rosabeth Kanter visited one shared household and asked who the group's leaders were. Everybody got named as a leader at one thing or another, including "John [who] leads us in drinking and having a good time." Shared households recognize the expertise that a member has in a particular area — say in gardening, or home repairs, or paying the mortgage installments and taxes. This is another way that decisions are made informally. At Napa House, our sixteen-year-old is an electronics whiz. He installs and maintains the extension telephones and the house intercom, making most of the decisions himself without having to consult anyone. Leadership of this sort works if everyone respects the leader's expertise in a particular area and the leader does not overstep the boundaries of that area.

Unilateral Decisions

Unilateral decisions go unchallenged in a member's room. Rearrange the furniture there ten times a day, and nobody will complain. Elsewhere in the house, some kind of consultation is usually necessary. One day a beautifully hand-lettered sign appeared inside the front door at Napa House, advising visitors to remove their shoes. Our guests found this odd, since only one of us—I'll call her Rose—walked around without shoes. She had posted the sign without checking with anyone else. Eventually it was removed. Recently, another of our members bolted a speed bag (a small punching bag used by boxers to develop agility and balance) to one of the redwood trees in our back yard. Because she hadn't checked with anyone, this move created resentment. There were complaints about the appearance of the frame that held the bag, and she was obliged to paint it. Then there were complaints about the noise that she made hitting the bag, and she was obliged to buy a quieter bag and to weight down the frame. After that, everyone was happy and now she bats the bag without a care in the world. But she would have had an easier time in the beginning if she had consulted the others before acting. Such a course would have shown them that she cared about their feelings and preferences and would have won her more willing cooperation.

People who live communally find they must pay attention to how they make decisions. This is partly a matter of good human relations. Housemates need to feel heard. They appreciate being consulted and resent not being consulted. But there is a deeper reason why members need to pay attention to how decisions are made. If an important decision is made unilaterally or by some members but not all, the whole method by which the group governs itself is called into question. Members begin to doubt whether they are actually equal. They begin to lose faith and trust in one another. When a household is set up to be run by consensus, it is important that members make sure this actually happens.

Although it is important to pay attention to the decision-making process, it isn't necessary to become bogged down in trivial, legalistic decision making. Some issues need to be settled in a house meeting, and many people think it's a good idea to have one every week. But house meetings don't have to be overly time consuming. When people feel heard and respected, they usually reach a consensus quickly. And many decisions don't have to be made in a house meeting at all. They can be made by asking around or by recognizing a member's leadership in certain limited areas. The greatest number of decisions to be made in a commune involve house-keeping, cooking, shopping, childcare, and other domestic matters. How commune members manage their domestic life cooperatively is the subject of the next chapter.

6. COOPERATIVE HOUSEKEEPING

In a traditional family, one person — the housewife — is normally responsible for cleaning, food shopping, and cooking. Many housewives are also expected to take charge of furnishing the house and of making arrangements for overnight guests. In a shared household the role of housewife disappears. Cleaning, cooking, food shopping, and so on are accomplished cooperatively, with everyone sharing equally in the work. The only exception is childcare, which remains largely though not entirely the mother's responsibility.

The strong belief in equality mentioned in Chapter One explains why there are no communal housewives. Because everyone is equal, it becomes necessary to divide the work equally among all members. The housewife doesn't simply disappear, however; she is replaced by everyone's cooperative efforts.

Commune members have learned an essential fact about cooperative efforts: Without some degree of organization, they are sure to fail. This doesn't mean that there is any "right way" to organize housekeeping tasks or that everything must be structured. On the other hand, every successful household has created some organization, and it isn't hard to see why. Without any structure, the least-liked chores — such as cleaning the bathroom — cause insurmountable problems. Either nobody does this work or certain people (often women) do more than their share and become deeply resentful. Structure ensures that housework gets done and that it is equally divided among all members — not just in theory but in practice as well.

One Berkeley commune was started by five people in their twenties who believed they wouldn't have to organize anything. In the beginning they cooked by rotation, and this was the only structure they had. Gradually and inevitably, they acquired more. Some members ate lunch or a snack and washed their dishes before leaving the kitchen. Other members left their dishes in the sink for the cook to wash that night. After a few months of this, the people who washed their lunch dishes began to feel they were doing more than their share and the others were taking advantage of them. This was discussed in a house meeting, and everybody agreed to wash their own lunch and snack dishes and not leave any in the sink. The next issue was raised by the women, who were unhappy because one member, Phil, never vacuumed or dusted or straightened up the house. Phil explained that he did all the gardening and paid all the house bills and assumed that in return for this the others were happy to clean. The women replied that they didn't enjoy cleaning as much as Phil had thought and would like to learn how to garden. The group decided that everyone would do some gardening and some cleaning and would have one bill to pay. That structured the gardening, cleaning and bill paying. It was not as easy to live without organization as they had expected.

HOUSEKEEPING

Some parts of the housewife's role are easier to accomplish cooperatively than other parts. Cooking is simple. True, men who haven't cooked must learn the job, but they usually appreciate the opportunity. And most people find that cooking is fun when they only have to do it once a week.

Cleaning is harder. Groups usually must invest a number of house meeting hours to arrive bit by bit at workable standards of cleanliness that will be observed by everyone. Does the person who cleans the bathroom mop the floor, or just sweep it, or not bother with the floor? How often should the bathroom be cleaned in the first place? Does cleaning the living room mean simply vacuuming, or does the person who cleans the living room also dust the furniture? And what about the dishes: Is it okay to leave them in the sink?

How Groups Decide on Housekeeping Standards

Cleaning is a complex issue because there are so many details to decide and because people have different standards of cleanliness and neatness. In a shared household the goal is to harmonize these differing standards and create a communal standard that satisfies everyone. This communal standard cannot be imposed by any one person, since everyone is equal, so it can be difficult to agree upon. But I prefer arriving at a communal standard democratically to having one person give orders, which is what most of us grew up with.

In one commune, some members grew up in "clean" families and others grew up in "messy" families, so when they first lived together their personal standards were incompatible. Eleanor, a housewife before her divorce, had a compulsive attitude about having everything clean and neat at all times. Two of the men were also divorced and had done little cleaning in the past. Eleanor explains what happened as the members of this group discussed cleaning in house meetings:

> I learned that other people didn't even see things that bothered me very much. They weren't deliberately trying to bug me — it's just that some people are accustomed to

more clutter and dirt than I am. It truly doesn't bother them. The others understood me better, too. They saw that I was genuinely uncomfortable with clutter and dirt, that I wasn't just complaining to hear myself talk. The result of all this is that now I've relaxed a lot and I can accept more disorder. The others have changed too. Now instead of vacuuming and thinking the job is finished, the men clear off the clutter on tables and dust the furniture.

The changes that Eleanor describes didn't happen overnight. It took the members months to fully explain what they wanted and why they felt as they did. But the results justified the effort: In the end, they arrived at a set of housekeeping standards that everyone supported.

How Groups Assign Chores

Some households have an intriguing way of persuading members to clean. Every six months or every year, they devise a new and ingenious method of assigning chores. The new system inspires everyone to do housework, and for the next six months or a year everything gets done. Then people become tired of doing chores, and it's time to inaugurate another ingenious system. I suspect that members of these households associate doing chores with parental authority. After they have been doing a chore for a while, they feel someone has ordered them to do it. Then they need to be reminded that there isn't any authority figure breathing down their necks saying, "You've got to put the garbage out!" When they think up a new way of doing chores, this provides the needed reminder that the members themselves are in control and have deliberately chosen to do housework.

Every group works out its own way of defining chores and deciding who will do them. There are obviously many ways to do this, but some methods are more commonly used than others. Some of these methods are described here, to give you an idea of how many communes organize their housekeeping.

Rotated chores. This is a good way to distribute jobs people don't like. Suppose nobody likes to clean the bathroom, and that you have six people and two bathrooms. Rotate the bathroom cleaning, and each member has to do it only once every three weeks. Other jobs, like vacuuming or emptying the garbage, can be rotated, too. An easy way to do it is to write the names of all members on a paper plate and mount the plate on a piece of cardboard on which the different chores are written. Each week when the chore wheel turns everyone gets a new job. Rotating chores is particularly appropriate if members want to learn how to do tasks that traditionally belong to the opposite sex. Putting bathroom cleaning and lawn mowing on the same chore wheel ensures that all members will get practice doing both.

Fixed chores. A "fixed chore" is one that the same person does every week. The advantage is that some people enjoy certain tasks, and would rather do them than rotate through all the jobs. Some people like to vacuum and others like to straighten up the living room. One way to assign fixed chores is to have everyone write down their first, second, and third choice. In the best of all possible worlds, all members will get chores they like. The problem with this system is the unpopular chore. I haven't met anyone yet whose favorite chore was cleaning the bathroom. Some groups work this out by assigning popular chores to the people who like them and rotating the unpopular jobs. Fixed chores are not fixed forever, of course. Eventually someone tires of one job, and trades with another member. Periodically there may be a general reshuffling of all chores, so that all members wind up with new ones.

Family chores. This method is used in some communes that are made up of nuclear families. Chores are assigned to each family, rather than to individuals. In a commune formed by two families, one shopped and cooked for a week and the other took over the following week. A commune formed by three families traded off every day: At the beginning of the week, each family chose the days it would cook and clean up. Assigning chores this way gives couples and families something to do together, reinforcing their separate identity within the group. This system also enables couples to retain some traditional sex roles if they wish to do so. For example, a wife could do the cooking every time it was her family's turn.

Sign-up lists. This is a way to remind people that they are choosing to do housework and that it isn't forced on them by some authority figure. All the chores are posted in the kitchen, and members write their names next to the chores they want to do during the coming week or month. Of course, there is a firm expectation that everyone will choose a job. Sometimes members don't sign a list until after they have done their chore. In one commune, a "dish list" is posted over the sink and members sign it after they wash the dinner dishes. Members determine when it is their turn to wash by counting the number of signatures since they last signed.

Work parties. These are a bit like old-fashioned barn-raisings: Everyone pitches in at once and works until the project is completed. Housework can actually be fun done this way. Work parties also are well adapted to major projects, such as painting a room, that would be too much for one or two people working alone. Some groups make sure that everyone pitches in enthusiastically by thinking up a way to reward themselves when the work is done. One group spent a day cleaning windows, cupboards, and closets; then they trooped off to a friend's houseboat for a party arranged in advance. I know of another group that does routine cleaning en masse and has a wonderful time. But most groups can't, because members' schedules are too different.

Work teams. This is another way to make work fun by enabling people to work together. A chore is assigned to a team of two or more members. Larger households often assign two people to cook together or to wash dishes together. In one of these communes, dishwashing is the most popular chore because of the companionship it affords. Because it is easier to find two people whose schedules fit than it is to get everyone together at once, work teams are easier to arrange than work parties, so they can be used for the daily routine jobs rather than the occasional major projects.

Hiring a maid. Some communes attempt to end their cleaning problems by hiring an outsider to clean. I know at least one commune that has a live-in maid. This group can afford maid service because each couple in the group has a substantial income. In most households, some members don't have a lot of money and aren't willing to pay for housekeeping—especially since many hands make light work in a commune, so members aren't required to devote much time to cleaning. But groups sometimes decide that there are one or two jobs that they don't want to do themselves. For example, one group that had a house with magnificent hardwood floors hired a woman who came a few hours a month to wax the floors and did nothing else.

How Groups Resolve Cleaning Disputes

Many nuclear families engage in periodic arguments about cleaning—especially if the wife has been influenced by the women's movement and her husband resists taking on household duties. Cleaning is a frequent source of friction in communes, too. The communes that I know of have found four ways to prevent or resolve cleaning disputes. First, these groups make sure the work is evenly distributed among the members. Second, they don't discuss housework in vague generalities— when necessary, they get down to details. Third, they don't allow men to shirk chores with the excuse that cleaning is "women's work." And fourth, they are aware that housework disputes can sometimes be caused by emotional conflicts that have nothing to do with housework.

Distribute the work evenly. In some households one or more members expect the others to do most of the work. This quickly produces resentment. Sometimes a self-sacrificing member chooses to do more work than the others for a while. But members who sacrifice soon begin to feel that they are the servants of the rest of the group and become resentful. Since resentment results when members do less than their share and when members do more than their share, the solution is easy: Everyone is happiest when the work is distributed evenly.

Some households manage to distribute the work evenly without a great deal of structure. At Napa House, for example, we rotate some chores, but we don't decide in advance who will repaper the kitchen shelves, clean out the refrigerator, mow the lawn, or perform similar jobs that need doing at irregular intervals. Instead, when it's time to do one of these jobs, someone volunteers in our house meeting. Because we meet every week, everyone knows who volunteered last, and which members might be expected to volunteer for the next job. Occasionally members forget to volunteer — and are reminded that they haven't done any extra jobs for a while. This informal process keeps all of us up to date on the work others are doing, and enables everyone to see that the work is evenly distributed.

Be specific. Although housekeeping entails a great number of little decisions, there is a strong temptation to save time in house meetings by glossing over these troublesome details. "I'd sure like to see things cleaner around here!" a member will say. "So would I!" chime in the others. Then the discussion moves on to something else. At the next house meeting, some members are angry. "I thought we all agreed to have things cleaner, but nothing happened!" they complain. The reason nothing happened is that the group didn't specify what needed to be done. At a Napa House meeting, a member fumed about "how dirty the house was getting." When we pinned him down, he discovered that he had only one complaint: The stove needed cleaning. It was

cleaned that week, but nothing would have happened if
he had stuck to generalities. Vague pleas for "more neatness" or "a cleaner house" aren't effective. People have
to specify the cleaning they want to see done.

Confront sexism. Sometimes a male commune member agrees only in principle to share the housework. In
practice, he puts off his chores, does a half-hearted job,
or forgets entirely. Confronted with these derelictions,
he may resort to sexist evasions. Pat Mainardi has
catalogued some of these dodges:

> "I don't mind sharing the housework, but I don't do it
> very well. We should each do the things we're best at."
> MEANING: "... I don't like the dull stupid boring jobs, so
> you should do them."
> "We have different standards, and why should I have
> to work to your standards? That's unfair." MEANING:
> "... Eventually doing all the housework yourself will be
> less painful to you than trying to get me to do half."
> "Housework is too trivial to even talk about." MEAN-
> ING: "... My purpose in life is to deal with matters of
> significance. You should do the housework."

Confronted alone, men find it easier to take refuge in
evasions like these. That's why women often use a house
meeting to raise male consciousness about housekeeping. With other people present, the women have
more support and men are forced to examine their own
behavior.

Sometimes female members discover that they have
been helping men avoid their share of the work. This
happens when women fall into the habit of cleaning up
after men who make messes. In one household the
women did this—and periodically became so resentful
that they refused to do any cleaning at all. When the
members understood it, this pattern was broken. Instead
of cleaning up after men, the women reminded men who
left a mess to clean up after themselves. The men soon
started doing it on their own.

Confrontation is not always the answer when men do

a poor job of cleaning. Sometimes a man is perfectly sincere about wanting to share the work equally, but doesn't know how to wax a floor, for example, and is shy about asking for instructions. Somebody gives him a short course in how to do the job, and the problem is solved. Women, too, need to learn tasks traditionally performed by the other sex. One group wanted to share all the work equally but the women, having no experience in lawn care, realized that they could make mistakes. The lawn could turn brown, whereupon the men might argue that only men could care for it properly, and that since men would be doing all the yard work it would be only fair for the women to do all the cleaning. So the women asked that the men help them learn how to care for the lawn.

Check for deeper conflicts. Sometimes when a husband and wife fight over who should take the garbage out, the issue really is the garbage. On other occasions, a housework dispute may be a symptom of a conflict that a couple doesn't fully recognize. So it is in shared households. Some cleaning fights are about cleaning, and some are really about something else. Dennis Jaffe believes that continuing friction over housework is often "a sign of deeper conflict around commitment (to the group), intimacy, or personal needs and boundaries." Rather than deal directly with this deeper issue, members feel safer fighting about housework.

Researcher Susan Dun, who has observed the functioning of many communal households, visited a group where a member—I'll call him Frank—was in the habit of serving dinner an hour late. In a house meeting, Frank was confronted with this. At first he made excuses: He had to run to the store for a forgotten ingredient, the stove didn't work right, and so on. Then a member said, "I've really got the feeling, Frank, that by making dinner late every time you're trying to tell us something." At last, Frank offered the real explanation. He felt that the others saw him as their resident "clown." It was true that he enjoyed making people laugh, but somehow it had gotten out of hand. Everyone seemed to think he was a happy-go-lucky, irresponsible person, and he resented it. The others understood and resolved to take Frank more seriously. From then on, he got dinner to the table on time.

"Frank's way of getting people to pay attention to his problem was to serve dinner late," Dun comments. "It was then up to them to decipher what the real problem was. This is a classic family dynamic." Instead of trying to guess the real problem, the members had the good sense to raise the issue in a house meeting and encourage Frank to identify it himself. When a housekeeping problem is a symptom of a deeper conflict, this is usually the best way to discover the source of the problem and resolve it.

MENU PLANNING, FOOD SHOPPING, AND COOKING

Food is important in a communal household—not only because people have to eat. The sense of family is often strongest when everyone sits down to dinner together. Contrast this with the feeling of eating alone, and it is easy to see one reason why people enjoy communal living. Each household develops its own ways of keeping the house stocked with groceries, of planning (or not planning) meals, of accommodating different diets, of paying for communal food, and of keeping communal and private food separate.

Meals: Planned and Unplanned

Meal planning in communal households ranges from nonexistent to informal to highly structured. "We don't have any scheduled dinners," a member of one group explains. "If someone happens to be in the kitchen cooking, that person may ask how many others want to eat." This is, needless to say, a group of quite independent people who like to eat when they are in the mood. In another commune, interest in dining together ebbs and flows. "We go through periods of maybe two weeks' duration when people get intrigued with cooking and we eat together a lot," a member says. "Then, for the next couple of weeks, it might be two fried eggs and a kind word."

At the other end of the spectrum are the households where everyone considers it essential that a communal meal be prepared five nights a week or even six or seven nights a week. There is no expectation that every member will be present for dinner five or seven nights a week, however. A member who has an evening class, a night meeting, a dinner date, or any other evening engagement is perfectly free to miss dinner with no questions asked. On the other hand, there usually is an expectation that a member won't consistently be absent from dinner.

There is a practical reason for this expectation. A member who is rarely present to eat with the others may, quite understandably, lose interest in cooking for them. Then, if it is a house where people expect to have a regular communal meal, the meal system begins to break down. When a new commune is being formed, therefore, it's an excellent idea to agree on how many nights a communal meal will be prepared, or to agree that there will be no scheduled dinners.

People who like to eat when they are in the mood view groups with regular communal meals as too regimented. Naturally, people who live in groups that eat together regularly don't share this view. They point out that an efficient system of meal planning, shopping, and cooking gives members more time to use as they please. A member of one group states the case like this:

> I know that every night Monday through Friday a meal will be served at 6:30, or just about then. This means I can be gone all day doing what I want to do, and get home at 6:30 and have dinner. This makes a lot of free time for me.

I never have to worry about going out and buying food, or about cooking, except on the days when I've signed up to shop or to cook.

To this person, a structured meal system means greater personal freedom.

Food Shopping

At Napa House we barely organize our shopping. We have a blackboard on which we note items that are running low, in the hope that someone will buy them. But we don't designate anyone to act as shopper, or expect anyone to shop on a particular day, or plan our menus in advance. We do expect everyone to spend approximately fifty dollars a month on food, since that's how much we all contribute to the shopping kitty. Our nonsystem works because there are several nearby supermarkets so it's easy for people to stop and shop if they are driving by anyway. Households with a more structured meal system usually appoint a different member each week to act as shopper. Members plan the meals they will cook and hand their individual shopping lists to the shopper, who spends an hour or two at the supermarket and returns with seventy or one hundred dollars' worth of supplies. There are many variations on this scheme. One household has a regular shopper who buys only staples like salt, flour, and coffee. Everything else is purchased by anyone who wants to shop.

Paying for food. Just as there are different ways to shop, there are different ways to pay for food. Groups on a tight budget often have each member contribute a fixed amount each month and then strive not to spend more than the total. In early 1979, some groups like Napa House that consume little meat were eating well on a contribution of fifty dollars a month per person. In households where members are less budget conscious, the amount spent for food varies each month.

By far the easiest method of paying for food is to assume that some people will be absent from dinner one night, others will be gone another night, and in the long run everything will even out. By this reasoning, it makes sense for everyone to contribute equally. However, some households have members who frequently eat away from home and others who are consistently present for meals. These groups sometimes collect a fixed amount for each meal actually consumed, even though this requires record keeping and calculation.

Many communes save money by buying food in bulk. Some households belong to food cooperatives that require members to donate their time to running the co-op. In San Francisco, a number of communal households belong to a co-op that makes weekly home deliveries and requires no volunteer work. For this service the co-op charges above wholesale, but still sells food at a substantial saving. If you haven't bought in bulk before, decide how you will store large quantities of food. Otherwise spoilage may erase your savings.

Private food. In nearly all communal households members buy some food privately, such as candy bars, liquor, imported delicacies, and items not on the communal shopping list. In some households, each member has a shelf for private items. Groups that have two refrigerators sometimes designate one as the communal refrigerator, meaning that anything inside can be eaten by anybody. The other refrigerator holds private items.

It may sound strange to have private food in a commune, where sharing is one of the reasons for living together. But everyone has favorite foods, and commune members have learned by experience that it helps to have a clear understanding about which items are communal and which are private. Sharing is fun when you have a six-pack and voluntarily offer a beer to a housemate. But coming home and discovering that an unidentified member has taken three of your beers is no fun at all. In some households, there is confusion about which items are private because everything must be shelved together.

This confusion can be alleviated by labeling private items with a bit of tape or a felt-tip pen.

Special Diets

Living communally provides an opportunity to learn new recipes and to enjoy new dishes and different styles of cooking. Last week at Napa House, one member made New England fish chowder, another made a Mexican dinner, and a third prepared a Chinese meal. Before I lived communally, I could cook scrambled eggs and TV dinners. Now I cook curry, quiche, frittata, shark steak, crêpes, and tamales — to list just a few specialties. Living with people who enjoy eating anything and everything is a broadening experience — in more ways than one.

Members of other communes choose to eat a more restricted diet. For example, many people are vegetarians. At Napa House, we aren't vegetarians but we try to eat "natural foods" most of the time. We avoid buying prepared foods that contain chemical additives, we try to limit our sugar intake, and we rarely buy red meat for communal meals, although it is perfectly all right to cook a hamburger for lunch or a steak on the weekend, when there is no communal dinner.

Many households accommodate a wide range of dietary preferences. Vegetarians and omnivores coexist happily in many communes. In one group, a cook who makes a meat dish prepares a vegetarian one as well. In another household, the vegetarians remove chunks of meat from their portions of stew: "We're all flexible and understanding about food, and our system works fine," a member explains. The one thing to avoid is living with people who want to force their preferences on others. A former housemate, for example, complained bitterly that the sugar smell made her sick when I baked cakes — and expected me to adopt a healthier diet. This kind of conflict can be averted by agreeing in advance on what dietary restrictions, if any, will be enforced in your household. At Napa House, we don't make cakes for the group, except on birthdays. But members who want to make their own private cakes are free to do so.

CHILDCARE

For parents, the chance to share childcare tasks is one of the big advantages of communal living. But the number of tasks shared varies widely from one commune to the next. In many households, parents wish to maintain close bonds with their own children and so perform the most intimate childcare activities themselves, such as bathing their children, reading to them in the evening, and putting them to bed. In other households, adults take turns performing these tasks.

Baby-sitting can be shared informally. A parent who is going out for the evening asks at dinner whether another adult is staying home and would be willing to watch over the kids. Later, the favor is reciprocated. Other groups use a sign-up sheet to make sure that one adult will be available to baby-sit each evening. One group consisted of six adults, four small children, and a teenager. Each adult worked four days a week and had house duty one day a week. While on house duty the adults cared for the kids, did their chores, and often prepared a gourmet dinner for the members who worked that day. Another group that had a number of kids and plenty of space hired a teacher and became a small daycare center. A few additional children were recruited from the neighborhood to make the operation economical.

Judith Blanton points out that groups need to reach a common understanding about baby-sitting. Some people consider being with children a privilege that is adequate reward in itself. Others view baby-sitting as a chore that, while not terribly disagreeable, deserves compensation. Parents can take turns baby-sitting, but a nonparent may want to be paid. It is essential to clarify these points when a new commune is being formed, and when a new member is recruited to join an existing household. Some groups find it helpful to discuss periodically how everyone feels about childcare. The discussion may reveal that a parent wants more help but is afraid to ask for it, that nonparents want to help but haven't said so because they are afraid that their offer will be rejected, or that nonparents feel guilty because they imagine that parents want more help.

Differences in Childrearing Style

Differences in childrearing styles need to be recognized when a group is being formed. If too little common ground exists, the parents should consider finding other adults to live with. For example, some parents firmly believe it is wrong to require children to do chores, while others are just as certain that kids should be made to do chores. This difference proved impossible to bridge in one household where adults resented cleaning up after one set of children who didn't do any housework. Although extreme differences are hard to overcome, child-rearing styles that are not completely divergent can be made to mesh. The group can adopt a "community standard" that all members are willing to support, although this isn't always necessary. Some differences can simply be accepted.

Accepting Differences

One father in a household with small children restricted the number of hours that his kids could watch TV. Another father allowed his children to watch as long as they liked. The two fathers explained to the whole group that they had a difference of opinion, and that the children would be expected to follow the wishes of their respective parents. Interestingly enough, this arrangement wasn't questioned by the kids and it worked. If the children had rejected the plan as unfair, it would have been necessary to agree on a community standard stating that all kids could watch TV for a certain number of hours per day.

In another commune, one set of parents made their kids eat eggs, bacon, or some other source of protein at breakfast. Another set of parents were satisfied if their children had only cereal and orange juice. The whole group discussed this. The parents said they had strong feelings about what kids should eat for breakfast, and acknowledged that two sets of parents disagreed. The children accepted this and ate what their respective parents wanted them to eat.

Creating Community Standards

When differences in childrearing style cannot be accepted, a community standard is in order. One group with small children decided that all the kids could play in the neighborhood after school—but they would have to check in at home first. Another community standard specified certain streets where kids were allowed to ride their bicycles. One commune had a parent who didn't worry about what his son ate—the boy could refuse vegetables and have hot dogs or hamburgers when he didn't like the adult menu. The children of two other parents were required to eat whatever the adults ate and didn't get dessert unless they ate their vegetables. These children decided that they were treated unfairly and the problem was discussed at length. Eventually everyone agreed to a community standard: All children would have to eat what the cook served, and kids who didn't eat their vegetables couldn't eat dessert.

Correcting and Punishing Children

Conflicts can arise between a child and an adult who isn't the child's parent. Suppose a child has turned up the TV volume to the annoyance of an adult, or a child is pestering an adult for attention. Most parents who live communally feel that in situations like these the adult should raise the issue directly with the child, rather than going to the parent. The adult can tell the child to turn down the TV or to stop pestering. This approach is the easiest and usually the most successful. Only if dealing directly with the child fails do parents want to be brought into the discussion.

Communal groups have found that it helps to discuss how far nonparents can go in correcting children or punishing them, so that everyone operates on the same basic assumptions. Is it okay for a nonparent to tell a misbehaving child, "Go to your room"? In some households, only a child's parents may invoke punishments. In other households, any adult may do so. Either system works. The important point is to be sure everyone agrees on which system will be used, and what the limitations of each member's authority will be.

Helping Parents Who Are Caught in a Bind

Parents all know the small child who goes into a tantrum and won't stop. But parents who live communally don't have to be stuck in this bind. "My daughter was throwing a tantrum every morning about getting dressed," a mother told me. "I talked to Elaine [another mother in the group] and she said, 'Why don't you let me take care of dressing her?'" When Elaine dressed the child, there were no tantrums. "Parent and child are so involved emotionally that it's easy for kids to manipulate a parent," says a family counselor who lives communally. "Kids usually act better with other people, and that's why it's possible for parents who live communally to take turns getting each other out of binds with their children."

Communal living does not, of course, enable parents to disengage themselves from all of the emotional strains of parenting. But sharing childcare can help with specific problems, such as the morning tantrum just described. As suggested in Chapter Three, living communally can also assist parents who see themselves as "overprotective" or "too controlling" and who want to give their children more independence.

FURNISHING THE HOUSE

Decorating her home "in good taste" was part of the traditional housewife's role. The new shared houses tend to be furnished more informally. Members who have furniture or rugs or draperies "donate" these items to the household. A living room may boast a French provincial couch, a colonial chair, a Moroccan hassock, and an Indian rug. Perhaps I exaggerate slightly, but the truth is that new communes tend to be furnished in an eclectic style that would not be featured in *Better Homes & Gardens*.

Furnishing a house with donated items doesn't cost anything—that is the great advantage. However, as the years pass certain drawbacks become apparent. Most items are donated only so long as the owner remains in the group. If Sally moves out, she may take the dining table with her, since it's hers. When this happens, the members often get together and buy a dining table that will be permanent house property. Also, furnishings eventually wear out and need to be replaced. Established communes often have replacement funds. Everybody pays a few dollars a month into the fund, and glassware or a piece of furniture or a new washing machine purchased with this money is communal property.

An additional way of replacing or adding to furnishings is the practice of giving gifts to the house. This is an established tradition in one household, especially at Christmas. Last year one member gave a living-room chair, another gave a set of plates, and a third gave a fireplace poker. Sometimes when gifts are given to the house, members do not give personal gifts to one another. But in some households members do both.

I know of a few groups that have instituted user fees to replace furnishings. This could not be done with a living room couch, but one group put a coin box on its washer. When the machine needs replacing there should be enough accumulated revenue to buy a new one.

Since donating is the most popular method of furnishing a house, I want to add a word of caution about items that need special care. Cast-iron frying pans are a good example. Many people haven't used these pans and are unaware that they rust instantly if they aren't dried after washing. Anyone who donates a cast-iron frying pan must warn everyone about how to care for it. One woman donated some crystal glasses that had sentimental value and then stayed awake at night worrying that they would be broken. Finally she realized she had made a mistake and withdrew the glasses from communal use. Now she donates an item only if she won't be upset if it wears out or breaks.

GUESTS, WELCOME OR NOT

In the last chapter I mentioned a household that tired of putting up guests who kept reappearing and staying for unspecified lengths of time. Eventually this commune adopted an official guest policy to protect itself against future visits by unwanted guests. There are at least three reasons that communes adopt guest policies. First is the fact that some visitors do not understand that a commune is a private home. Given the opportunity, they will treat a commune as though it were a hotel and restaurant and stay around until somebody ejects them. Second, guest policies prevent disputes among members of the group. Without a policy, it is possible for one member to invite guests and insist that they stay for long periods, even though other members find the guests obnoxious. Third, some members are so unassertive that they can't say no when friends or even strangers request permission to stay. Backed by a communal guest policy, unassertive members say no with ease.

Groups need protection against guests, but they also

want to guarantee the right of all members to invite guests. Fortunately, communes have evolved a guest policy that reconciles these two potentially contradictory goals. All of the established communes that I know of have roughly the same policy, as follows:

1. Nobody can visit or stay overnight without an invitation from a member of the household.

2. Without consulting anyone, a member can invite a guest to stay for a limited time (in some communes for one night only, in others for two or three nights).

3. If a member wants a guest to stay longer, everyone must be consulted and must agree before the host issues an extended invitation.

This policy works well in practice. If a friend from out of town shows up unexpectedly and needs a place to stay, there usually isn't time to check with all members. So the host is authorized to issue an invitation without consulting. A host who wants to issue an extended invitation has the next day or two in which to check with the other members. Most households hold the host responsible for explaining the policy to a guest, and for explaining other household agreements as well, such as the distinction between communal and private food, recording of long-distance telephone calls, any rules about smoking in the house, and so on.

Guests' Food

Communes pay in a number of ways for food that guests eat. When we have dinner guests at Napa House, no one contributes anything extra to the food kitty. We assume that in the long run all members will invite approximately the same number of guests, so there is no need to bill one another for the food they consume. Other households require the host or the guest to put an extra dollar in the kitty to pay for the guest's food. Guests who stay for a week or longer do contribute to the food fund at Napa House. Most communes follow this practice. In some households guests who stay this long contribute to housing costs as well. At least one commune has created an "associate member" status for guests who stay regularly for three nights or longer. An associate member, who may be a member's lover, relative, or child, pays twenty-five dollars for a three-night stay and forty dollars for five nights.

The theme running throughout this chapter has been how people living communally share household duties, food, childcare, belongings, and responsibility for guests. Usually these aspects of everyday life are viewed as mundane and uninteresting. Everyday life in a communal household is anything but mundane—it is an exciting adventure. Sometimes, when people disagree, this lifestyle is exasperating. But it is often fun, and it always provides a strong feeling of involvement with other people. The next chapter is addressed to people who want to participate in this adventure: It explains how to join an existing commune and how to start a new one.

7. GETTING STARTED IN SHARED LIVING

If you want to start living communally you have two choices: You can join an existing commune or start a new one. Depending on where you live and what type of shared household you want to be part of, it may be possible to locate a group that already exists in your community and to join it. To do this successfully, you need to be clear about the kind of living situation you want and to know something about the process that communal households use to select new members. There are several ways to start a new commune and a number of questions to be answered before a group of people decide to live together. A checklist of these questions appears in this chapter.

JOINING AN EXISTING HOUSEHOLD

Making Connections

You can track down a commune that has a vacancy with a minimum of detective work. If you want to join a commune, tell your friends. One of them may know of an existing group, and groups feel safer recruiting a new member who comes with the personal recommendation of someone they know. You will also want to check the bulletin boards where households advertise for new members. In Berkeley, for example, the bulletin boards at the Co-op supermarkets list scores of communal vacancies. There is also probably a community information center of one kind or another in your town. The information centers I have in mind include women's and men's centers, centers sponsored by churches and community organizations, and centers run by people interested in personal growth or alternative lifestyles. Information centers like these usually have their own bulletin boards and may have lists of communes that have vacancies. Some centers that provide this information are listed in Appendix A, along with national organizations and publications that list communes with vacancies. Alternative newspapers carry classified ads announcing vacancies in communes, often under a "shared living" heading. University housing services and roommate referral bureaus are still other sources of information.

Clarifying What You Want

When you locate a commune in your community with a vacancy, you could just go there and talk to the members, and perhaps they would invite you to join. But your chances of being invited will improve if first you clarify in your own mind what you want. People who live communally are not impressed by candidates for membership who aren't sure why they want to live communally or why they aren't satisfied with their present lifestyle. Candidates should know how they feel about structure: Are they looking for a group of people who take no communal meals or who eat together five nights a week? Are they interested in living with children? And so on. You don't need to come up with a firm answer to all such questions. But giving these matters some thought will improve your chances of making a good impression when you visit a communal group.

Being Interviewed

Strangers who drop in unannounced are no more welcome in a shared home than in any other private home. The best way to make contact with a group is by telephone. As will be explained in the following chapter, which outlines the entire selection process from the group's point of view, you will probably be asked preliminary questions (do you smoke? do you have pets?) when you call. If you pass this screening you will be invited to come to the house at a convenient time.

Upon arrival you will normally be given a house tour and you will be interviewed, either quite informally or in a more structured fashion. If the interview is informal, you will probably chat with one member at a time, learning something about each person and the household and telling each person something about yourself. If the process is more formal, you may meet with everyone at once. This can be a somewhat nerve-wracking experience: The members take turns asking questions while you, inwardly a bundle of anxiety, try to come across as friendly and relaxed. Whether you are interviewed informally or formally, be sure that *you* ask questions, too. This is the time to continue clarifying what you want and to discover what the group wants. Find out what is expected of members: Do they attend regular house meetings? Communal dinners? How does the chore system operate? People will be more interested in you if you show an interest in them. And they react more positively to candidates who are able to relax and be themselves.

One of your reasons for visiting is to evaluate the group. Do the people you are meeting seem distant or depressed? Is the kitchen a complete mess? If so, you may want to find another household to join. But if you are favorably impressed and your visit has gone well, you will probably be invited to return later in the week to talk some more, perhaps over dinner.

Being Selected

Each candidate is interviewed in turn and the process of selection can last more than a month. Under these circumstances, all you can do is be patient and call back at intervals to remind the members that you are still interested in their group. If you are rejected, remember that candidates are vetoed for many reasons. Perhaps you reminded a member of her despised Aunt Agatha. Maybe you came across as quite intelligent, and someone found that too threatening. Being rejected does hurt: The important thing is not to get discouraged. You are bound to have better luck elsewhere. I was turned down by three groups before I found my present home at Napa House. Many people go through similar experiences before they are accepted into a commune.

STARTING A NEW HOUSEHOLD

Starting a new commune is a creative act. The first links are forged in a chain of human relationships that stretches into the future. This section describes some common methods of commune founding and explains the issues that people will probably want to discuss before they decide whether to live together.

Exploratory Discussions

A commune is made, not born. Usually one person or, better yet, two or three take the initiative. For the purpose of exploratory discussions, the initiators bring together a group of people interested in communal living. There are various ways to find these people. Maybe you have friends or co-workers who would like to live communally, and perhaps they in turn have friends who would be interested. Often people who want to found a commune start with friends and then reach out to more people through the organizations they belong to or through the community information centers and other communication channels described at the beginning of this chapter. In this way a group of people can be brought together in a reasonably short time.

There are also long-range approaches to finding people. Some individuals join social or political or other organizations partly to meet others they might want to live with. A friend of mine is the cofounder of an organization that conducts personal growth workshops, and in this capacity he meets thousands of people a year. "My entire life's work," he says, "is casting a net to pull in interesting people." If you view living communally as a project that may take months or years to accomplish, you can make a point of getting to know people, writing down addresses and telephone numbers, and keeping in contact with them.

Another ambitious way to find people is to start an organization that will help people find compatible individuals to live with. Such an organization, called Building Expanded Families, was founded in 1974 in San Jose, California, and continued until 1977, when the volunteer staff ran out of energy. At meetings of this group, people interested in living communally were clustered according to the type of commune they wanted to start. Participants met with one cluster and then another until they found others they liked who had similar expectations. When enough compatible people came together in this way, they looked for a house to lease or buy. About fifteen households were formed during the life of the organization.

However your group is formed, your meetings will progress depending on how well people know one another. If everyone knows each other quite well, you might announce that the purpose of the first meeting is to plan a commune. But often exploratory meetings bring together some people who are only acquaintances or who are meeting each other for the first time. If this is the case, people will want to find out whether their values, expectations, and personalities are compatible before they decide to live together.

One commune almost stopped before it started because the people who attended the exploratory meetings assumed that everyone would be included in the commune. The initiator of these meetings was a California widow who brought together a dozen people, many of whom did not know one another, to consider starting a communal household. After several months of meetings, nine seriously interested people remained. Four wanted to live together, but did not want to live with the remaining five. Because it had been assumed that everyone would automatically be included, the four couldn't summon up the courage to tell the others, "We don't want to live with you." Instead they announced that they didn't want to live communally after all, and the discussion group disbanded in apparent failure. Later the four got together by telephone. They decided to recruit more compatible people and went on to found a highly successful commune.

If people don't know each other well, it is a good idea to stress that your exploratory meetings are aimed at the formation of one or more households. This way if only some prove to be compatible the others need not give up the idea of communal living entirely. They can form another commune, or they can bring in more people and continue exploratory discussions until a second group of compatible people has come together.

Few shared households are formed overnight, although I do know of three married couples who needed only two days to decide to live together. Other people meet once a week for several weeks or months to become acquainted and to compare expectations. Meeting in someone's home helps to establish a friendly atmosphere; dinner meetings, especially potlucks, are popular. Sometimes a group goes camping together early in the process of forming a commune. Some people know that they like each other when they first meet. Other people may need to meet several times before they know each other well enough to be sure they want to live together.

Retreats and Trial Runs

Comparing expectations in a discussion meeting is extremely helpful, but people who hope to live together often take additional steps to test their compatibility. They go off on group retreats or live together on a trial basis. These tests may reveal important information that does not come out in discussion. Parents who live communally sometimes complain that an adult or another child plays too roughly with their children or sets an example the parents don't like. When a group spends a day or longer together, parents can observe how everyone behaves with their kids.

Retreats. A camping trip is one way to go on retreat. One group rejected two people after everyone had camped together for a weekend. The first person mooched others' food but wouldn't share her own. The second was a "helpless" type who wouldn't tackle any task without assistance. Groups that don't like camping can rent a vacation house for a few days. Sometimes a member who owns a large house invites everyone to move in for a weekend. One group decided that they wanted to spend a whole summer getting to know one another and discussing the household they would like to start. To make this possible, everyone got jobs as counselors at the same summer camp. By fall, they were certain that they would enjoy living together.

Trial runs. There's a possibility that people will be on their "best behavior" when they are together for only a weekend or that conflict that didn't show up during a short retreat will become evident when people live together. Some groups arrange to live together in a rented house for six months or a year, on a trial basis. Trial runs are particularly attractive to people who own houses that they are reluctant to sell without assurance that they will like living communally. Homeowners can rent their house to another family for the period of the trial run, so that at the end of the trial they have the option of returning to their house or selling it and investing some of the proceeds in a jointly owned communal house. One group of eight people took a six-month lease on a house with an option to buy. At the end of this trial period, three people dropped out. The other five bought the house and continued to live there communally. The three New York families whose commune is described in Chapter One initially rented a beach house for the summer. "By the end of the summer," they reported, "we knew we had found the people and the pattern we wished to make permanent."

GETTING OFF TO A GOOD START

As I pointed out in Chapters Four and Five, people learn to be more assertive and self-aware when they live communally. If you want to speed up this learning process, consider using a facilitator—a psychologist or other professional trained to help people interact effectively in small groups. One new group hired a facilitator to attend their first house meetings. When members failed to listen to one another or to communicate clearly, the facilitator pointed this out and advised the group on how to communicate better. By the time the facilitator had attended seven meetings, the members had learned to communicate well and her services were no longer needed. Perhaps because it started so well, this group was unusually successful: No one left for the first three years. Facilitation is not for everyone, since some people view psychologists and other group process experts with suspicion. But if the members of your group are open to the idea it is worth considering.

COMPARING EXPECTATIONS: A CHECKLIST

Making sure that people like one another is important, but you will also want to be sure there is enough common ground on which to found a household. This means exploring differences as well as the things that bring you together. The goal is to make sure there are no extreme differences that would make living together unwise. Discovering that some people have seriously conflicting expectations concerning closeness, sex, or childrearing will enable you to subtract and add prospective members until you have assembled a group that can live together harmoniously.

By discussing the questions that follow, people can determine how compatible they are. So this checklist can be used not only by a group that contemplates forming a commune but also by an existing commune that is interviewing prospective new members and by an individual interested in joining an existing household.

For a group that intends to live together, answering these questions can start the process of planning a household. In most instances, the purpose of discussing a question will not be to reach any specific agreement but merely to check for differences. For illustrative purposes, however, the right-hand column lists agreements that some households have made or that could be made. The middle column indicates in which chapter or chapters the questions are discussed.

Closeness and Shared Interests

Members of some communal groups share a particular interest, while other groups are built on a diversity of interests. Some people may want the whole group to participate in activities outside the house, but others may not be interested in this kind of togetherness. Some people may look forward to the intense closeness produced by open sharing of feelings, while others may want companionship and a sense of community without much personal sharing. One way to become close is to use communication or encounter techniques—but some people may be strongly opposed to these methods. Expectations concerning sexual behavior may also vary widely. These differences must be revealed before a group commits itself to living communally.

Question	Where Discussed	Possible Agreement
Will we expect all members to share a common interest?	Chapter Two, sections on shared-interest and multi-interest households	We want all members to be interested in _____. Or: We expect to have a diversity of interests.
Will we expect everyone to participate in a project?	Chapter Two, section on shared-interest households	Members may launch projects but there is no obligation to participate. Or: We all agree to participate in the following project: _____.
Will we expect everyone to participate as a group in activities outside the house?	First part of Chapter Three	We expect members to participate in the following outside activities: _____. Or: We have no expectations concerning outside activities.
Will we expect members to	Chapter Four	We want companionship and a sense

Question	Where Discussed	Possible Agreement
share feelings and details of their private lives?		of community. If members grow close we will welcome that, but we don't expect it. Or: We expect members to share their feelings and experiences openly.
Will we use encounter or communication techniques?	Chapter Two, section on growth households; Chapter Five, sections on creating a favorable climate for consensus and no-lose problem solving; this chapter, preceding section on getting off to a good start	We agree to use the following techniques: _____. Or: We aren't interested in using group process techniques.
What are our expectations concerning sex?	Chapter Three	We agree that there will be no sex across couple lines. Or: We want to experiment with non-monogamous sexual arrangements, as follows: _____.

Decision Making

Everyone who lives communally agrees that house meetings are important, at least occasionally, but there is disagreement about whether it's necessary to hold regularly scheduled meetings. It's a good idea to reach a specific agreement on whether they will take place regularly. House meetings become more necessary as the size of a group increases. People may have different expectations about the size of your group and about what might constitute overcrowding. One way to prevent both overcrowding and unnecessary disputes is to set a policy on admission of new members. It is wise to agree on this policy in advance.

Question	Where Discussed	Possible Agreement
Will we have regularly scheduled house meetings?	Chapter Five	We agree to meet every Wednesday and we expect everyone to attend. Or: We agree that any member can call a meeting at a time convenient for all. When a meeting is called, we expect everyone to attend.
How many people do we want to live with?	Chapter Four	We agree that the number of members will not exceed the number of bedrooms. Or: We agree that couples or children may share a room.

Question	Where Discussed	Possible Agreement
Under what circumstances will new members be admitted to the household?	Chapter Four; Chapter Eight, section on the final decision	We agree that no one will move into our house without the unanimous approval of all members. We will not accept a candidate whom all members have not met prior to our decision.

Domestic Arrangements

You can't work out all the details of your housekeeping system in advance. But you can make sure you are in accord on basic principles. You can check to see if everyone agrees that the housework should be shared equally, with the men doing as much work as the women, or if people have other ideas. You can also check for extreme differences concerning organization, since some communal households are much more structured than others. Groups often prefer to maintain an equal number of male and female members—in part so that the special talents of both sexes are available—so you may want to discuss whether such a sex balance will be your goal. You will want to find out whether differing dietary preferences are represented in your discussion group and whether they could be accommodated if everyone were living together. People may have divergent expectations about guests, so this topic is worth discussing, even though groups often do not adopt a guest policy until they have been living together for a while.

It is wise to be specific about certain uses of the house. Some people don't want to live with anyone who smokes tobacco. Others would ban marijuana from their house. Pets are another potential source of disagreement: Some people are attached to their pets, but others are allergic to animals. What if someone wants to hold band practice in the living room, repair cars in the back yard, or use the dining room to hold growth workshops? You can prevent disputes by finding out whether anyone might want to use the house for a special purpose and deciding whether the use will be allowed.

Most people who live communally are quite responsible financially. But occasionally someone joins a group hoping to be supported by the others. You can avoid any possibility of misunderstanding by discussing what members' financial obligations will be.

Question	Where Discussed	Possible Agreement
Will we share the housework equally? Will men and women do equal amounts of work?	Chapter Six	We agree to share equally in the work of shopping, cooking, cleaning, and caring for the yard. Or: We choose to retain some traditional sex roles, as follows: _____.
Will we develop organized ways of house-keeping?	Chapter Six	We will define chores and assign them to individuals by rotation or in some other organized way. Or: We will coordinate our housekeeping

Question	Where Discussed	Possible Agreement
		activities in weekly house meetings. Or: When members see the need to clean something, they will clean it.
Will we eat together regularly?	Chapter Six	We agree that a communal meal will be prepared on the following nights: _____. Or: there will be no communal meals. Members will eat together whenever they feel like it.
Are people unwilling to eat certain foods, to have certain foods purchased with communal funds, or to have certain foods prepared in the house?	Chapter Six	As long as we stay within our food budget, members can purchase anything that strikes their fancy and serve it at communal dinners. Or: Certain foods, namely _____, will not be purchased with communal funds, although members are free to buy any kind of food pri-

Question	Where Discussed	Possible Agreement
		vately and prepare it in the house. Or: We won't allow certain foods, namely _____, to be prepared in the house.
If there are meat-eaters and vegetarians in our group, will it be possible for them to eat together?	Chapter Six	We agree that when meat is served, vegetarian dishes will also be served.
Approximately how much are we willing to spend on food?	Chapter Six	Our food budget, at least initially, will not exceed $___ per month. Or: We want to eat well and we aren't greatly concerned about how much it costs.
Will we develop organized ways of shopping?	Chapter Six	We agree to rotate the shopping. Or: Shopping will be done informally.
Do we want an approximately equal number of men and women in our group?	Chapter Two	As far as possible, we will maintain a balance of men and women. Or: When we have a vacancy, we will choose the

Question	Where Discussed	Possible Agreement
		best candidate regardless of sex.
Will we have any rules about guests?	Chapter Six	We agree that no guest may stay overnight without an invitation from a member of our household. Without consulting anyone, a member can invite a guest for ____ nights. A host who wants a guest to stay longer must obtain the agreement of all members.
Will we allow tobacco smoking in the house?		We will allow smoking anywhere. Or: Members may smoke in their rooms or on the porch. Or: We don't want to live with anyone who smokes.
Will we allow marijuana smoking in the house?		We will allow marijuana smoking anywhere. Or: Members may smoke marijuana only in their rooms or on the porch. Or:

Question	Where Discussed	Possible Agreement
		We don't want to live with anyone who smokes marijuana.
Will we have pets? What kind? Is anyone allergic to pets?		The pets we now own will become part of the household. A member who wants to add another pet must receive the group's approval. Or: We will not allow any pets in the household.
Does anyone want to use the house, garage, or yard for business purposes, to practice music, or for any other special purpose that might be of concern to other members?		The proposed use of the house is (is not) approved.
Does everyone have a job or some other reasonably reliable		We agree to pay our shares of the rent (or mortgage payments), utilities,

Question	Where Discussed	Possible Agreement
source of income? Does anyone expect to be helped out financially by the others?		food, and other expenses promptly and in full. We recognize the possibility that over the years we may grow to be such a close-knit family that some members will want to support others financially. But for the foreseeable future, we firmly expect all members to pay their share of our expenses.
What financial responsibility does a member who leaves the group have to the rest of us?	Appendix B	We agree that anyone who decides to leave will give as much advance notice as possible so that we can proceed in an orderly fashion to recruit a new member. We also agree that anyone who leaves without notice will pay a month's housing costs so that the others are not penalized.

Children

Some people want to live with kids, and others want to live with adults only. If everyone is in agreement that they don't want to live with children, you won't need to explore the question further. On the other hand, if some people have children or want to live with children, a number of questions will need to be answered.

Since parents and children tend to suffer in a commune where childrearing is merely incidental, you can check to see how much time and energy people want to give to children. When more than one set of parents live together, there are bound to be differences in childrearing style. This is one area where it is especially important to detect extreme differences that might be irreconcilable. A parent may be strict on one issue and permissive on another, so you will need to discuss specifics.

Question	Where Discussed	Possible Agreement
Do we want to live with children? Are we interested in forming a commune in which children will be a central focus?	Chapter Two, section on family communes	We agree that our household will be for adults only; no children will be admitted. Or: We would like to live with up to _____ [how many] children in the age range of _____.
Are any of us parents of children who live with a former spouse? If so, will these chil-	Chapter Four	We agree that a member's child is welcome to stay with us on weekends. Or: A member's child is

Question	Where Discussed	Possible Agreement
dren be welcome as regular visitors or as future members?		welcome to stay for up to one month at a time. Or: We agree to accept a member's child as a visitor and as a future member of our household.
Do we expect nonparents to become friends with the children? Roughly how much time do we expect nonparents to spend with the kids?	Chapter Three, section on finding people who like children	We do (do not) expect nonparents to establish warm relationships with the kids based on daily or almost daily interaction with them.
Do we expect nonparents to baby-sit, feed the kids, or care for them in other ways? Will nonparents be compensated for these tasks?	Chapter Six, section on sharing childcare	We expect nonparents to care for children in the following ways: _____, and we will compensate them as follows: _____. Or: We expect nonparents to care for the children in the following ways: _____, without compensation. Or: We don't expect nonparents

Question	Where Discussed	Possible Agreement
		to care for the children.
Will we require children to do chores?	Chapter Six, section on getting child-rearing styles to mesh	All children over the age of _____ will do chores tailored to the child's age and ability. Or: We agree that no child will be compelled to do chores.
Will children have a bedtime?	Chapter Six, section on getting child-rearing styles to mesh	We agree that children will (will not) have a bedtime.
Who may correct or discipline children?	Chapter Six, section on getting child-rearing styles to mesh	Any member may ask a child to stop intruding, but only a child's parents may discipline a child. Or: In the absence of a child's parents, any member may discipline a child in certain ways, as follows: _____.
Do we want to restrict the kind of TV programs	Chapter Six, section on getting child-	Children may watch TV whenever they feel

Question	Where Discussed	Possible Agreement
that children may watch or the number of hours per day that they may watch?	rearing styles to mesh	like it. Or: The following restrictions apply: _____.
Do we want to specify what children will eat?	Chapter Six, section on getting child-rearing styles to mesh	Children may eat whatever they want. Or: We agree to the following rules about what children may eat: _____. Or: Each parent or set of parents will decide what their own kids will eat. If this proves unworkable, we will decide on a set of community standards.

Back in Chapter One, I said that the communal-living lifestyle is available to almost everyone. In this chapter I have tried to explain how people who want to live communally can do so, either by joining an existing household or by starting a new one. As you have seen, neither process is guaranteed to be quick and easy. People who want to join a commune sometimes get turned down and must try another household that has a vacancy. Starting a new household often takes months. But people who want to live communally and are willing to invest some effort are rewarded with a strong sense of achievement—and membership a house that is full of new friends—when they succeed.

In this chapter the way that people join existing households was explained from the point of view of someone looking for a commune to join. The next chapter reverses the point of view to explain how communes that have a vacancy look for people, how communes deal with the changes that membership turnover brings, and how communal groups go about disbanding.

8. GOING THROUGH CHANGES

A shared household can be seen as a special kind of family. The members have modified the traditional family form to keep qualities they like, such as closeness and emotional support, and to get rid of qualities they dislike. They dislike irreconcilable value differences, such as those associated with the generation gap, and avoid such differences by choosing to live with people who have similar values. The members abolish the position of housewife and divide the housework equally. Rather than having decisions made by the "head of the household" or dictated by sex roles, they make decisions by consensus. Finally, the members eliminate the burden of family obligations by deciding that someone who no longer wants to be part of the household is free to depart and not feel guilty about leaving.

In traditional families there is a moral and even a legal obligation to remain a member no matter how painful family life becomes. But members of communes assume that someone who no longer wants to be part of the group is free to go. In place of an obligation to remain a member, communes substitute an expectation concerning members' behavior while they are part of the group. Members are expected to be open and honest with each other, to uphold their group's traditions and agreements, and to do their best to resolve any conflicts—for as long as they remain part of the group.

A member who decides to leave is usually replaced. If a new member were not recruited, those who remained would enjoy the companionship of one less person. Economic factors also dictate the decision to replace members who leave: If the group's size were allowed to decrease, each member would have to pay a larger share of housing costs. This chapter explains how communes cope with the emotional consequences of turnover and how they recruit new members.

Some middle-class communes become institutions that seem destined to last forever, despite the fact that over the years some of the original members leave and are replaced. I know a number of groups founded more than five years ago that are still going strong, since members are replaced as they leave. Other communes disband. This choice is open should the members decide that the commune no longer meets their needs.

TURNOVER

Members leave for many reasons. Transferred to a job in another city, a member may choose employer over commune. A single member who falls in love may give up communal living to live in nuclear fashion. Often people leave to join another household that fits their needs better. They may prefer the other group because it is less structured (or more structured) or because its members do more together (or do less together) or because it doesn't have children (or has children). One researcher, Ann Hershberger, interviewed people who were leaving communes and found that, of those with definite plans, the largest number expected to move to another commune.

Some people believe that turnover is necessary, especially in the first year or two of a commune's life. Accord ing to this theory, some members will inevitably discover that they have not joined the right group. When they depart, those who remain get a chance to build a more harmonious and cohesive group by selecting people whose expectations and personal styles are more like their own. Another theory is that after a year or two, a core group of about four or five members is established. The other members of the group may change every year or two, but the core group remains to provide needed stability and continuity. These theories don't describe accurately what happens in every commune, but they do describe some familiar patterns.

How Children Are Affected

Since small children can be hurt by the loss of someone with whom they are close, parents sometimes worry about the effect that turnover will have on their children. Psychologist Judith Blanton points out that kids who live in traditional families must also cope with relationships that periodically dissolve. "These children have teachers, day camp leaders, summer camp leaders — all people who are part of the child's life one day and apt to be gone the next," she says. One of Rosabeth Kanter's interview subjects, the divorced mother of two girls, made a similar point. She spoke of

> the great loss her daughters suffered in their pre-commune days, when the family with four young kids next door moved away and there was no one else at home to help cushion the blow. Now, in their "big family" of the commune, they feel sad when someone leaves but handle the loss with much less storm and stress.

According to this mother, kids who live in traditional families and kids who live communally both have to deal with relationships that end — and communal kids are better equipped to deal with the problem because they have other friends to cushion the blow.

Few social scientists have examined the effect of communal turnover on children, but one study reported in the medical journal *Pediatrics* addresses this question directly. The study dealt with twenty mostly rural communes in Oregon, Washington, and British Columbia. Nuclear families retained their identity within these groups, and 80 percent of the couples were married. The researchers observed seventy-four children and concluded that the only kids who suffered as a result of turnover were those few children who did not have a close or stable relationship with either parent. Rather than being hurt by the turnover, children who had a secure relationship with at least one parent experienced the departure of old members and the arrival of new ones as "positive stimulation." When a child's need for a secure relationship with one person is met, this study indicates that temporary relationships with other people in the commune may actually be good for the child.

Taking Departures in Stride

The last member of Napa House who left wanted to live with a man and eventually raise a family with him. Since we all know him well and her plans had been discussed with the group for more than a year, her departure was not a sudden shock. She parted on the best of terms and visits us regularly. If people communicate well, so that everyone understands why a member is leaving, the departure doesn't have to be at all unpleasant.

Two years ago when another member left there were some hurt feelings. This member was a musician who gradually became more and more involved with his friends in the music world, and less and less involved with his friends at Napa House. Eventually he was seen around the house only a few times a week and was almost never present for dinner. When the question of his withdrawal from the group was raised in a house meeting, he first reacted angrily and then promised to be around more. A few months later he decided to move out. It is fairly common for a member to move away from the group over a period of time. Sometimes the member withdraws because of a misunderstanding that can be uncovered and corrected. In our case there wasn't any misunderstanding. All we could do was point out that we didn't like what was happening and help our musician make up his mind to move on.

FINDING NEW MEMBERS

When someone leaves, a new member must be found. It helps to be in a positive frame of mind about this. Here is your chance to recruit an interesting, responsible person who will be fun to live with and will help you become a closer and stronger group. This is a better way of approaching the task ahead than dwelling on your worries about how well the new person will fit in. Of course it's not enough merely to expect that you will recruit a good person—usually you must take concrete steps to make this happen. Established communes have a somewhat orderly process for recruiting and selecting new members. A member who plans to leave gives thirty days' notice or more if possible. This gives the group time to launch recruitment efforts that begin with advertising the vacancy and end when a new member is selected.

Advertising

Members mention an impending vacancy to friends and acquaintances who may know of a good candidate for membership or who may want to be candidates themselves. If your group is part of a larger social network, you may want to advertise by word-of-mouth only. This is often practical if your members are active in local schools, church groups, political groups, or other community organizations. Perhaps there have been meetings, potlucks, or workshops at your house, in which case many people know about your commune. Some of them may be eager to join.

If you aren't part of a larger social network, you will probably need to advertise on bulletin boards or in print (see the preceding chapter's section on making connections and Appendix A). The more thought you put into an ad, the better chance you have of attracting the kind of person you want. Composing a good notice has another benefit: It helps you define the things that are most important to you as a group. However, if you define yourselves too narrowly you rule out too many prospective members. If you advertise for a man twenty-eight to thirty-five years old who doesn't smoke, likes kids, is interested in holistic health, and is a liberal Republican, you'll get few responses. On the other hand, if your ad is too vague you can waste time talking to many people who are clearly ineligible. The first ad below appeared in *The New Republic's* classified advertising section. The other two ads appeared in the *Communal Grapevine Newsletter* published in Oakland, California. All three ads describe the commune and the kind of person sought without excluding too many good candidates.

Family Commune

A small group of families living together now has an opening. We own our home, share expenses, not incomes — we all hold outside jobs. We're beginning our fourth year of vegetable gardening. We tend toward organic methods and healthful diet. Membership requires no initial monetary investment. Operating and food costs are billed monthly. If you are seriously interested in exploring community living as a more human life style, call us at 000-0000. On Friday nights we often have charades, poetry reading, or candlemaking. Saturdays — harvesting potatoes, building, or splitting logs.

Benvenue House

Benvenue House has space for two people, 25 years or older. We are currently three women, two men, and one cat (no more pets, please) living in a big old brown shingle house in Elmwood. We have a fireplace, small garden, deck, a few fruit trees, and lots of room. We enjoy sewing, quilting, fancy cooking, geology, dinnertime get-togethers, fantasy literature. We share cooking and chores and need only a fair amount of structure to keep things running smoothly. Person born on March 22, 1947, will be given special consideration! Telephone 000-0000.

Communal Household

We are an intentional family of three women and three men, age range 29-45. We are looking for a responsible third man to complete our communal household. We are a caring and sharing group, have evening meals together and weekly house meetings. We have a large older home with sundeck and vegetable garden. We like open communication and growth. Small room with bath available now, $115. Call 000-0000.

Screening Candidates

It's not unusual to have fifteen or twenty people apply to fill a communal vacancy. One suburban commune that advertised in a Boston newspaper had over two hundred replies, which must be a record. Communes use a telephone screening process to make talking to so many people less time consuming. A list of preliminary questions is posted by the telephone so that whoever answers will remember to ask, Do you smoke? Do you have pets or children? How old are you? Do you want to live in a house where we eat together so many nights a week? Candidates who pass the telephone screening get invited to see the house, meet the members, and be interviewed.

As I mentioned in Chapter Seven, interviews range from a friendly chat with each member to a more formal meeting in which all the members take turns shooting questions at a candidate. However you conduct your interview, you have two main goals: to find out whether you like the candidate as a person and to make sure the candidate understands what is expected of members of your group and is willing to make the necessary agreements concerning chores, meals, house meetings, and so forth.

Deciding whether you like a candidate isn't too difficult if you pay attention to your own reactions. One commune member explains how her group makes this decision: "It's like meeting someone at a party and knowing you want to get to know them better. When that chemistry isn't there, we pass over the candidate." Another woman with several years' experience in communal living notices a candidate's body language. "If he's comfortable being here, talking to us, that's good," she says. "Being uncomfortable may indicate that he isn't sure he wants to live communally." Some people who are unsure about communal living may stay for a month or two and move out; others who at first have doubts about communal living make exemplary housemates.

Some groups are particularly interested in recruiting members who are self-aware and are good communicators, on the theory that these qualities are necessary in communal living. One group puts the following questions to candidates: What do you imagine would be your strengths and limitations as a member of this household? What do you do with your time? What are your interests? Have you lived with other people before? What was it like? You may hesitate to ask questions that seem too personal. But you are choosing someone to become part of your home — someone whom you hope to establish a personal relationship with. Viewed in this light, few questions are too personal.

Communicate What You Expect

Sometimes people are careless about telling a candidate what the group expects of its members. The results can be fairly disastrous. Suppose, for example, that attendance at your Monday evening house meeting is required, or that equal sharing of the cooking and chores is essential. If your new member moves in believing that house meetings are optional or that it's okay to let the bathroom go for a couple of weeks without cleaning it, your group is in trouble. Perhaps the members were too unassertive to explain their expectations carefully when the new member was interviewed, or maybe everybody assumed somebody else had outlined your agreements. Sometimes new members aren't properly briefed because members of the group are unclear about what they expect. A group might, for example, have some members who view weekly house meetings as required and others who feel that scheduled meetings aren't so important.

One way to make sure candidates are told about your expectations is to sit down before you interview anyone and go over what you expect of one another. If members have different views, this is a good opportunity to arrive at a shared understanding of what you want to happen in your household. You may want to list your major expectations and decide on how they will be communicated to the candidates. One way is for the whole group to meet with the most promising candidate to review your expectations one by one, making sure you get a clear response from the candidate on each point.

Leveling With Candidates

You will probably have little trouble remembering to tell candidates the good things about your group — the nice back yard, the fireplace, the warm atmosphere at dinner, and so forth. But there are probably some drawbacks to living in your household: Maybe the room that's vacant is in a noisy location; perhaps two of your members haven't been getting along with each other. It is important to mention these facts too. Candidates who don't learn about drawbacks until after they have moved in may resent the fact that they weren't told sooner.

Overnight Stays

Sometimes a group invites a promising candidate to stay at the house for two or three nights in hopes of getting to know the person better. Even a brief stay can reveal important facts that may not come out in an interview. At one commune, a candidate made a good impression during a ninety-minute interview. Invited to stay overnight, she arrived much later than promised. Soon afterward, the telephone started ringing as friends and relatives sought frantically to get in touch with her. It became clear that she was leading a chaotic life that would have disrupted the household and this had not been revealed in the interview.

Trial Memberships

Many communes invite a promising candidate to stay for up to three months on a trial basis. This arrangement has obvious advantages to the group. At the end of the trial period, the members can feel reasonably certain whether they want to live with the person or not. Sometimes candidates aren't sure about a group and appreciate the chance to learn more by staying on a trial basis. When a candidate has this attitude, a trial membership can be quite successful. On the other hand, some candidates would rather look elsewhere than be admitted for a trial, which they view as an anxious period that may end in rejection and the necessity of moving again. For this reason, some communes have stopped requiring trial memberships.

The Final Decision

Sooner or later, a group has to make a decision on admitting a candidate. Most households have an understanding that this is an important decision which needs to be made with care. Therefore, no decision is reached until all members have had a chance to talk with the most promising candidate or candidates at least once, and the decision itself is made in a house meeting with everyone present. As mentioned in Chapter Four, the "veto system" is widely used—in fact, I don't know of any household that doesn't use it. No candidate is admitted without the approval of all members. There are disadvantages to this system. Sometimes a candidate liked by most of the members gets vetoed. Sometimes it is necessary to interview many candidates before one who is acceptable to everyone can be found. On the other hand, the veto guarantees all members that they won't be required to live with someone they dislike. The veto system also eliminates the possibility that a newcomer will be undercut by a member who was opposed to living with the person. Suppose that a group voted on candidates, accepting the one who got the most votes or a majority vote or a two-thirds vote. The members who voted no might accord the new member only grudging acceptance, rationalizing their behavior by asking, "Why should I like somebody whom I didn't want to live with and, in fact, voted against?" Consensus decision making —which is what the veto system amounts to—sometimes takes longer, but once the decision is made, everyone can be counted on to support it.

DISBANDING

Utopian communes often disbanded with a sense of failure. The members had built their lives around a cherished set of religious or political beliefs, only to discover that the new society they envisioned did not materialize. Members of a middle-class commune may be sad when they bid one another goodbye, but they do not need to feel that they have failed. They didn't set out to build a new society. All they wanted was a kind of alternative family or miniature community that would last as long as it met their needs.

Commune members know that their needs are likely to change over time—that the lifestyle that fits today may not fit five or ten years from now. Social scientists have documented the fact that not only children, but adults, too, pass through stages of growth. Thus a group of adults may find that communal living meets their needs for closeness or learning at one stage of life, and not at another. Under these circumstances, a decision to dissolve their commune is not an admission of failure, but rather a recognition of the need for change.

Separation Anxiety

When you live communally it's necessary to be sensitive to one another's feelings from the first day that the group is planned. The need to deal with feelings does not magically disappear when a group decides to disband. Instead, an extra effort to communicate fully may be required. Research done on encounter groups by psychologist William Schutz shows that members become anxious when their group is about to disband. A commune is not an encounter group, but members feel the same separation anxiety.

According to Schutz, members react to this anxiety in three ways. As the end comes closer, some people gradually withdraw their emotional investment in the group. They are absent more often and have less to say to the others. Another common reaction is to belittle the group. Members make disparaging remarks as if to say, "You see, I won't miss such an unimportant group." The third and less frequent reaction is to turn actively against the group. Schutz says a member who does this seeks to "shift the responsibility for separation onto the other group members by becoming antagonistic and forcing them to reject him from the group."

If you continue to hold regular house meetings or to communicate in other ways, separation anxiety can be resolved so that people will feel good about one another when they say goodbye. A practical reason for continuing to communicate is that important business matters may not yet be concluded. Large sums of money will be involved if the group owns its house. Although a written communal ownership agreement (see Appendix C) will help prevent misunderstandings or disagreements, the final real estate decisions will be more pleasant to make when members remain on good terms.

Looking Backward — and Ahead

Most groups that dissolve cope well with the anxiety that surrounds separation — members are good friends when they part. When members get together later, they have a lot to talk about. They look back on the years they lived together as a time of special warmth. Three families in Portland, Oregon, parted after living together for three and one-half years. I talked with Marie, one of the wives, as she was preparing to leave for California. "We all have it in our plans to live communally again," she said. "In fact, I'm leaning toward doing it in San Jose. There isn't one of us who would give up the experience we had, not one."

Her interest in living communally again is not surprising. The experience she would not give up was one of closeness with others, of learning, and of growth. Today the personal interaction that makes these experiences possible is hard to find. Because personal contact can be found in the communal households of the new extended families, people will continue to seek the rewards this lifestyle offers.

APPENDIX A:
DIRECTORY
OF RESOURCE
CENTERS
AND PUBLICATIONS

In cities across the country, lists of people who want to live communally and of households that are looking for new members are maintained by women's and men's centers, by churches, by food co-ops, by agencies that assist older people, and by other community organizations. These organizations are too numerous to list here. By making a telephone call you can find out whether your local women's center or food co-op, for example, has information about communal living.

This directory lists only organizations whose primary mission includes support of communal living. Most of the community information centers identified here maintain lists of people looking for communes and communes looking for people. They also sponsor discussion groups, workshops, and conferences for people who want to learn more about communal living and for people already living communally who want to share ideas on how to deal with common problems. Local information centers are listed first, followed by national organizations and publications that provide information about communal living and that, in most cases, help people who want to live communally contact one another.

LOCAL INFORMATION CENTERS

Arizona

Tucson. New West Trails Collective, 2237 E. 18th St., Tucson 85719. Telephone 602-624-9644 or 623-2003. Information on communal living. Resource library. Sponsored a 1978 conference on topics including the creation of communal households and how to deal with interpersonal conflicts in communal households.

California

Los Angeles. Communal Living Clearing Center, 3916 Inglewood Blvd., Apt. 4, Los Angeles 90066. Telephone 213-379-5355. Center planned to move as this book went to press. Permanent mailing address: Box 798, Manhattan Beach 90266. Listing service. Workshops on communal living. Sponsored by Family Synergy (see below under National Organizations).

Oakland-Berkeley. The Communal Grapevine, 1715 Gouldin Rd., Oakland 94611. Telephone 415-534-6076. A support and communication network of intentional families. *Communal Grapevine Newsletter* includes listings of households with vacancies and articles about communal living. Monthly discussions and potlucks.

San Francisco. Action for Better Living for Elders (ABLE), 1265 Fourth Ave., San Francisco 94122. Telephone 415-564-4468. For older people who want to meet others interested in communal living and start their own shared households.

San Francisco. San Francisco Communal Grapevine. No central office; mailing address: c/o RSVP, 681 Ellis St., Box 885, San Francisco 94109. Telephone 415-929-0671. A volunteer organization that encourages and supports communal living. Listing service, monthly discussions.

Connecticut

New Haven. Community Cooperative sponsors Wednesday night meetings for people looking for communal vacancies and communes looking for people. Meetings held at Down to Earth Restaurant, 96A Howe St. Telephone 203-562-3525. A card file of people and households is maintained at the restaurant.

Massachusetts

Allston (Boston). New Community Projects, 449 Cambridge St., Allston 02134. Telephone 617-783-3060. Listing service. Discussion groups. Informal counseling for individuals interested in alternative living situations. Weekly meetings for people looking for households and households looking for people.

Boston. Shared Living Project, 67 Newbury St., Boston 02116. Telephone 617-266-3814 or 266-2257. Sponsored by the Back Bay Aging Concerns Committee and the Gray Panthers of Greater Boston. Helps older people come together in shared living situations, including a communal house that is owned by the Aging Concerns Committee.

New York

New York City. Alternative Lifestyle Groups, 175 W. 12th St., #19A, New York 10011. Unlisted telephone number. Workshops for people interested in communal living and sexually open relationships.

Pennsylvania

Philadelphia. Act II Communities, 9803 Roosevelt Blvd., Philadelphia 19114. Telephone 215-332-7669. Local meetings and a semiannual conference on communal living for persons at midlife or older. Aim: to establish groups of persons past childrearing age who can live together through old age.

NATIONAL ORGANIZATIONS
AND PUBLICATIONS

Communities, Twin Oaks Community, Route 4, Louisa, VA 23093. A magazine, published six times a year, devoted to communal living, cooperative businesses, and related subjects. Lists communal groups, urban and rural, that are looking for people; lists people looking for groups. Subscription: Six dollars a year.

Community Service, Inc., 114 E. Whiteman St., Yellow Springs, OH 45387. Telephone 513-767-2161. Supports the development of new forms of family and community. Does consulting and research, publishes a newsletter, and distributes books about community and communal living.

Family Synergy, Box 2668, Culver City, CA 90230. Telephone 213-379-5355. No central office; activities conducted from members' homes in greater Los Angeles. Membership organization of persons interested in alternative lifestyles including communal living and sexually open relationships. Monthly newsletter. Sponsors many workshops and social events.

Mother Earth News, Box 70, Hendersonville, NC 28739. Monthly magazine. "Positions and Situations" column lists rural back-to-the-land groups looking for people and people looking for groups. Does not list urban communes.

Movement for a New Society, 4722 Baltimore Ave., Philadelphia, PA 19143. Telephone 215-724-1464. A national network of small groups working nonviolently for fundamental social change. Groups include communal households and work collectives. Groups in a number of major cities can be contacted through the central office in Philadelphia.

Older Women's Network, 3502 Coyote Creek Rd., Wolf Creek, OR 97497. Promotes the development of a network of feminist communities, mostly rural, for older women. Publishes a newsletter and a directory of members in nineteen states. Sponsors retreats and workshops.

Radical Psychiatry Network, 49 Hoffman Ave., San Francisco, CA 94114. A national network and support group of persons interested in radical politics and psychotherapy. Newsletter carries notices placed by communal households looking for people and people looking for households.

APPENDIX B:
RENTING OR BUYING
A HOUSE
COMMUNALLY

Some communal groups own their home and others rent. Buying a house is financially easier for groups than for individuals or nuclear families. Suppose eight people want to buy a house. If the downpayment is twelve thousand dollars, each person's contribution is only fifteen hundred dollars—and the monthly payments will also be split eight ways. Unfortunately, this doesn't mean that eight low-income people can team up to buy a house. Lenders would consider them unqualified to receive a mortgage loan, as explained below. This is why some groups rent—like many nuclear families, they can't afford to buy. Other groups could afford to buy but choose to rent during an initial trial-run period, as noted in Chapter Seven.

Groups are not always treated the same way as traditional families are by city officials, landlords, and mortgage lenders. The first section of this appendix discusses zoning—a matter of special concern to groups whether they rent or buy. Groups want a house that they will enjoy living in and that will attract new members. To this end, the location, the type of house, and how much the rent or house payments will be are important considerations. For groups that plan to rent, this appendix offers suggestions on how to persuade a landlord you will be good tenants, how to decide on the best lease, and how to apportion rent among yourselves. For groups that plan to buy, this appendix also discusses the advantages and disadvantages of ownership, how to qualify for a real estate loan, how to create a legal foundation for group ownership, and how to obtain insurance. If you do decide to buy, Appendix C covers another matter of importance: the communal home ownership agreement.

ZONING CONSIDERATIONS

Many cities restrict the number of unrelated adults who can live together in certain neighborhoods. Often the number of unrelated adults allowed in "single family" zoning districts is five; in some places it is eight. If you live in a metropolitan area, as most Americans now do, you will probably have to do some research to identify the municipalities and the zoning districts where communes are accepted and those it would be safer to avoid. If you live in an isolated town that bans communes in single-family zones, you will probably find that communes are allowed in higher-density residential zones. Some suburbs have only single-family zoning, but even in these places groups find houses where they can live without violating zoning regulations. They might find a house on the edge of town in a rural zoning district or a house in town that is covered by a preexisting zoning variance allowing group occupancy. Three Illinois families, for example, were legally entitled to occupy their home because it had been a fraternity house and had a variance when they moved in.

How Zoning Is Enforced

In some cities — for example, in San Francisco, Oakland, and Berkeley, California — more than five unrelated people are prohibited from living together in certain residential zones, but communes have existed in these zones in large numbers for more than six years without serious challenge. Communes were briefly challenged in Berkeley in 1978, when the city planning commission proposed reducing the number of unrelated persons who could live together to three. But the outcome was a major victory for people who live communally: More than one thousand commune members attended a City Council meeting to defend their way of life, and the Council unanimously rejected the proposed change. Across the country, the pattern of zoning enforcement varies from place to place. In some communities an ordinance discriminating against communes exists but isn't enforced. In some other places, restrictive ordinances are enforced only when neighbors complain. And in a few exclusive, upper-income suburbs, local officials actively search for violations of the zoning code.

To learn about zoning in your area and how it is enforced, you can check with zoning officers, city attorneys, or real estate agents. If you are interested in a particular neighborhood, you can knock on a few doors and find out whether communes already exist there. You will feel most comfortable living where it is obvious that discriminatory rules do not exist or will not be enforced. Some groups, however, take the risk of living where restrictions exist but are enforced only when neighbors complain.

Staying on good terms with neighbors. Groups that live where a neighbor's complaint could lead to enforcement of zoning restrictions naturally want to maintain good relations with their neighbors. One West Coast group impressed its neighbors favorably by organizing a neighborhood cleanup drive and becoming leading participants in the local block association. Groups can also avoid actions that might offend neighbors, and they can deemphasize their communal nature. The surest way to make neighbors irate is to take up on-street parking places where they have been accustomed to park. Allowing the exterior of your house to deteriorate, neglecting to mow the lawn, and sunbathing nude in public view are other ways to upset neighbors. You can downplay the fact that a number of unrelated people share a house by not listing everyone's name on the mailbox.

Dealing with inspectors. Newly formed groups can avoid serious legal difficulties by choosing a house where communal occupancy is allowed. Many existing households, however, are located where the law says they shouldn't be and their members have good reason to feel anxious when a city inspector shows up at their door. A city official who lives communally explains how some groups have reacted to an inspector's visit. First, they found out how old the complaint was. If it was several months old, the inspector was likely going through the motions of investigating and hoped the group would help close the case. One group stated calmly that only five people lived with them—although it was true that they had had some visitors recently. The inspector usually didn't launch the time-consuming investigation required to prove how many people were permanent occupants of the house. Some communes do survive by dealing with inspectors in this way, but they pay a stiff price: The members must live with the knowledge that if city officials decide to enforce the law, their group could be forced to leave its home.

Discriminatory Zoning Is Unjust and Self-Defeating

Discriminatory zoning grows out of prejudice against groups that are different from traditional families. As the average citizen becomes aware of what communal households are actually like, we can expect fewer discriminatory ordinances. Several years ago the elderly members of the first Share-A-Home commune in Winter Park, Florida, were accused of violating a local zoning ordinance that defined a family as "one or more persons occupying a dwelling and living as a single housekeeping unit." Judge Claude Edwards of Florida's Ninth Circuit Court visited the group and ruled in their favor. "I went out and saw they were living as a family and as a single housekeeping unit," he said. "I was delighted to see that it was a happy, well-run family."

Zoning that makes it more difficult for people to choose how they will live is not merely unjust. It is also self-defeating, because rather than preserving older neighborhoods, discriminatory zoning promotes their deterioration. Few of today's small nuclear families can afford to rent or buy the large older homes that were built for the extended families of past generations. In many communities gracious older homes have been partitioned into jerry-built apartments, allowed to run down, or demolished and replaced with new apartment buildings. But in other communities older neighborhoods have survived intact because communal families occupy the houses. With more breadwinners than a nuclear family, groups can afford to buy and maintain large houses or to pay enough rent so that decent upkeep is possible. Provided they are not banned by zoning ordinances, communes can make it possible to preserve whole neighborhoods.

Groups can help to preserve suburban neighborhoods as well as urban ones. An elegant house stood deserted in a New York suburb in 1972 because it was so big it had to be priced beyond the reach of most families. The three families who make up the first commune described in Chapter One teamed up to buy it. In so doing they rescued it from deterioration and also prevented a decline in the value of the adjoining homes. But they were forced to ignore a local zoning ordinance that made their rescue operation illegal. Signing themselves the "Elm Lane Eight," this group wrote a *New York Times* article stating the case for more flexible zoning:

> We hope that people who write ordinances, and neighbors protective of property values, will view housing uses on a performance basis.... Let's have ordinances

about parking, sanitation, and other material effects on the community. We could pass any reasonable criteria in these respects. But let's also allow people to expand their lifestyle options and, at the same time, enhance older housing that is underused.

The Elm Lane Eight went on to say that they do not object to rules ensuring adequate parking or to health regulations that prevent jamming so many bodies into a house that it becomes a threat to public health. But they do object to zoning rules that allow nuclear families of any size to occupy a house, while arbitrarily telling families that aren't related by blood or marriage that they aren't entitled to live together.

CHOOSING A HOUSE

Picking a Good Location

If your group is newly formed, you may not wish to consider the possibility of membership turnover. The experience of most middle-class communes, however, is that over the years some members leave and are replaced. Communes that are in or near urban centers usually have the largest choice of new members when they need to recruit them. An attractive outlying location can also be successful, but inaccessible locations should be avoided. If many people are uninterested because getting to work would take too long from your house, you may have to settle for replacement members whom you would otherwise reject.

What Type of House?

Groups usually prefer older houses because they have the most space, cost less, absorb more sound, and feel more like a home. Most groups choose a house large enough to provide a private room for every adult member, although children sometimes share a room. Many houses have a den, attic, basement, or garage that can be converted into an additional bedroom. Groups get more for their money if the architectural plan allocates most of the interior space to bedrooms or rooms that can be used as bedrooms. If the house has large common rooms and tiny bedrooms, the rent on each bedroom may have to be set too high in comparison with other communal houses in your community, causing problems if you need to recruit new members. An older house with thick, sound-insulating walls is preferable to a modern house with thin walls, and if the bedrooms are on separate wings or floors, noise problems will also be reduced. On the other hand, bedrooms located next to the kitchen, living room, or dining room may be very noisy.

Deciding What You Can Afford

Living together is less fun if you stretch your finances too far. After living communally for a while some members may want to quit nine-to-five jobs and live on reduced incomes, but this may be impossible if the group is locked into high rent or mortgage payments. Another problem can become apparent when you need to replace a member and the rent that must be charged for the vacant room is high. In calculating what they can afford, groups that buy a house are usually careful to estimate what home maintenance and repairs will cost. Often a reserve fund is set up to cover these costs and everyone contributes a few dollars to it.

RENTING

Renting can be either a short-term or a long-term arrangement, depending on what considerations are most important to a group. Groups that rent don't have to produce large sums of money for use as a downpayment and, as already noted, may prefer renting during the "trial run" of a new household. Another advantage of renting is that it avoids the time-consuming bookkeeping work that is part of owning a house communally (see the next section). A disadvantage to renting is that the group doesn't acquire equity in its house, as happens when a group owns its home. Another disadvantage is the insecurity of knowing that when the lease runs out, the landlord could sell the house.

Persuading a Landlord to Rent to You

In communities where communal households are common, some landlords are eager to rent to groups. These landlords are the owners of houses that are too large to attract nuclear families. Where middle-class communes are not so well known, a group may have to work harder to gain a landlord's confidence. It may suffice that your members look like responsible adults and have good credit ratings. But one good way to impress a landlord is to walk in with a neatly typed fact sheet listing each member's name, occupation, income, and credit standing. You can also point out that renting to a group with multiple incomes is safer than renting to a family with only one or two breadwinners who might quit or lose their jobs and fall behind in the rent. Occasionally a group tries to deceive a landlord by picking one or two members to sign the lease, pretending that they will be sole occupants of the house. But misrepresenting yourselves is risky: If the landlord finds out you could be evicted.

Getting the Best Lease

The best lease, if you can get it, may be for one year, with an option to renew, or for a longer term. Sometimes a group rents a lovely house and settles into communal life when the owner returns from a stay abroad or in another state and decides to reoccupy the house. A two-year lease is more secure and makes it psychologically easier to become close and to invest more in fixing up and decorating the house. Another possibility is the commercial lease, which has a long term and can enable a group to feel as though it owned the house. One San Francisco commune held such a lease for several years, functioning in effect as its own landlord. The group was responsible for paying property taxes and insurance premiums, for carrying out all routine maintenance, and for spending a specified amount each year on permanent improvements. The commune had full discretion to decide what improvements to make, and members could contribute their labor in lieu of paying for these improvements. This group has now gone one step further — it has bought its house.

Making Financial Agreements Among Yourselves

People living communally for the first time tend to view what they are doing with unbounded idealism. They believe that they are living together to share as much as possible and that making agreements about money would be unspeakably crass. After they gain a little experience in communal living, their attitude changes. They still believe in sharing — for example, they regularly lend each other small amounts of money and are happy to do so. But they realize that a member who falls behind in the rent is "borrowing" from the others without permission. Groups don't tolerate this kind of behavior because the members understand that warm, familylike feelings must be built on mutual trust. This basic trust erodes quickly when a member is financially irresponsible or when there are disagreements about money matters.

To prevent disagreements, groups that rent clarify what the members expect of one another financially. Most groups agree that a member who decides to move out will give the others thirty days' notice, or more if possible. A second agreement specifies that a member who fails to give notice will be responsible for paying thirty days' rent. These two agreements ensure that the group will have time to recruit a good replacement member and will not have to absorb the lost rent contribution of a member who leaves without giving adequate notice. Usually a third agreement clarifies what will happen if a room is vacant for more than a month so that rent is lost: The members all contribute equally to make up the loss.

Apportioning the rent. Groups must decide how to divide the rent among themselves. Usually each room is assigned a rent based on its size and sometimes on other factors, such as whether it has a private bath. This system enables high- and low-income people to live together. It is quite common to have one or two members with limited incomes occupying the smallest bedrooms, contributing one hundred dollars a month or even less to the rent. Members with larger incomes take the master bedrooms, for which they might pay one hundred fifty dollars a month. This arrangement makes everyone happy. The more affluent members are pleased because they get the large rooms, and the poorer members are pleased because they can afford to live in a nice house.

BUYING

The decision to buy a house is not made casually, whether the buyer is an individual, a traditional family, or a group. Too much money is at stake, and many pros and cons need to be weighed. For communes, as for nuclear families, home ownership holds both advantages and disadvantages.

Advantages of Ownership

Money paid as rent can never be recovered. But when you accumulate equity in a house, you have the option of selling it and converting your equity back into cash. Communal ownership agreements (see Appendix C) provide for this. Groups also find greater security in home ownership—there is no risk that their house will be sold to a new owner who will evict them. A group that owns its home can invest time and money on repair, redecoration, adding rooms, or making other improvements. A strong sense of unity and involvement with the group usually results from these home improvement projects. Even if you don't make improvements, ownership alone can contribute to group cohesion. "We are all equal owners of this house," one commune member says proudly. "We all have a stake in it."

Disadvantages of Ownership

A group that buys a house should be prepared to do some fairly complicated bookkeeping. Members are entitled to federal income tax deductions based on their individual contributions to mortgage interest and to property taxes. These amounts must be carefully calculated and recorded. It is also necessary to record the amounts each member contributes to home repair and improvement. These figures will be needed if the house is sold—both for income tax purposes and to determine what portion of the sale price each member receives.

Groups also need to make provision for the possibility that a co-owner will decide to move out. Perhaps the co-owner's share of the house will be purchased by the replacement member, or perhaps the other members will buy the share. Then there will be no problem. But if everyone has a modest income and cannot afford to buy the share, the group is in a dilemma. Either the departing member must agree to have the money tied up in the house for a time, or the house must be sold. Some groups provide for this problem by specifying that a member who leaves can be repaid in installments (for the wording of such a provision, see Appendix C).

Accommodating Income Differences

Many groups consist of members with both high and low incomes. Fortunately, it is easy to accommodate these differences when a group buys a house. If two or three members have substantial incomes, they can contribute the bulk of the downpayment, while the others contribute smaller amounts. Just as when a group leases a house, each room is assigned a rent. The higher-income members take the larger rooms and pay a larger share of the house payments. The lower-income members take the smaller rooms and pay less. If and when the house is sold, a member who has invested two thousand dollars in the downpayment receives twice as much as someone who has invested one thousand dollars.

Income differences are unlikely to cause any problem when all or most members contribute something to the downpayment. However, if just one member or one couple makes the major contribution to the downpayment, it becomes important to clarify expectations beforehand. Will the person or persons who make the major contribution expect to have more power in deciding, for example, how the house will be decorated and maintained, or how rooms will be used? If so, this needs to be spelled out in advance, perhaps as part of your communal ownership agreement. What happens when one member or couple is sole owner of a communal house is discussed in Appendix D.

Qualifying for a Real Estate Loan

A nuclear family that wants a real estate loan must meet two basic qualifications: The family must make a substantial downpayment and must have an income high enough to convince the lender that monthly house payments will be made on schedule. Communal groups must meet the same requirements.

Often a group has three or four high-income members who apply for the loan. The lender combines their incomes to decide how much they are qualified to borrow. Although the names of the other members may not appear on the loan, the communal home ownership agreement (explained in the following section and in Appendix C) makes clear that all members of the group are obligated to repay it. In recent years lenders have become accustomed to doing business with groups. Two or three couples or three or four unrelated individuals are usually able to get a loan with no more difficulty than a single family.

But lenders still follow some restrictive practices. More than four unrelated individuals will probably find that they cannot combine their incomes to meet a lender's income qualifications. This unwillingness to consider the combined incomes of more than four people makes it impossible for a group of low-income people to qualify for a loan. Suppose that five people, each of whom earns around five thousand dollars a year, want to buy a house. Their combined income is twenty-five thousand dollars—easily enough to get them a loan if they were a nuclear family. But the group would be turned down.

Nonetheless, groups of low-income people do sometimes manage to buy a house. If the members have saved a large amount of money, they may be able to qualify for a loan by making an unusually large downpayment. Sometimes a parent of one of the members advances a large sum as a downpayment, or cosigns the loan (a cosigner agrees to be liable for repayment of the loan if the group defaults). Another possibility appeals to groups with an appetite for hard work: They can buy a run-down house and rebuild it. Such houses can be acquired for free in some communities under government-sponsored urban homesteading programs.

Legal Forms of Communal Ownership

A group must create a legal foundation for joint ownership of its house. Since middle-class communes aim to be a union of equals, one way to proceed is to create a corporate entity controlled by the group as a whole. Such an entity might be a trust or a nonprofit corporation, which becomes the legal owner of the house. Unfortunately, trusts and nonprofit corporations are expensive to set up: Legal fees may be five hundred dollars or more. Furthermore, corporate entities must meet periodic filing requirements that will add to your bookkeeping load. For these reasons most communal groups do not form a trust or incorporate. Instead, they buy their house by means of a conventional real estate transaction and supplement the transaction with a communal ownership agreement.

Real estate transaction-communal ownership agreement. A group that takes this course buys a house, usually with the help of a real estate agent, and simultaneously drafts its own communal ownership agreement. Appendix C is a guide to drafting this agreement, which specifies how large a share each member owns, explains how shares may be transferred, and answers a number of other important questions. It is important to have the draft agreement inspected by a lawyer, who may suggest improvements before you sign it.

Your communal ownership agreement can remain a private contract or it can be filed with the local recorder of deeds, along with the deed to your house. Your lawyer and the real estate agent who sells you the house and helps to arrange the loan can advise you on whether to file the agreement. You will all become owners of record if the agreement is filed or if you are all named in the loan and deed.

Suppose that some names are not recorded and that the members have a serious quarrel five years hence. The three or four members whose names are on file as the owners of the house could conspire to sell it, pocket the money, and leave town before the rest of the group discovers what they have done. If everyone is an owner of record, this scheme could never be carried out.

And yet, groups often do not make everyone an owner of record. Sometimes the real estate agent knows the lender is conservative and doesn't like dealing with groups, so the lender is allowed to assume that the only owners are the three or four persons whose names appear on the loan application. Other groups have a different reason for not recording the names of every owner: They occupy their house in violation of zoning laws, and don't want to create written evidence of this fact. Groups that do not record every name don't consider that they are taking an undue risk. The communal ownership agreement does name all of the owners and it is a legal contract that can be produced in court if necessary. The advice of one real estate lawyer who helps groups buy houses is this: If you can record everyone's name without upsetting the lender or zoning officer, by all means do so. Otherwise, record only some names.

At some point one of the members whose name appears on your loan may decide to leave, and you will want to sell the ownership share to a replacement member. A few years ago, you probably would have been required to notify your lender and perhaps even take out a new loan. Recently the law has begun to change, so that now it may not be necessary to notify your lender. But to find out the proper procedure, it is necessary to consult a lawyer whenever you wish to transfer a share.

Real estate trusts. The members of a communal household can be simultaneously the donors, trustees, and beneficiaries of a trust. As legal owners of the property, the trustees are required to manage it in the best interest of the beneficiaries. Your lawyer may suggest naming only some members as trustees — not the whole group. But another section of the document can state that the trustees may act only with the agreement of all members, ensuring that you will be a union of equals. One group that chose to organize as a trust owned a house in the city and a piece of country land. They were able to place ownership of both properties in a single convenient entity — the trust. Although a trust can be drawn up and put into effect much more quickly than other forms of corporate ownership, a lawyer must do the work, which is too complex for a layperson. Another disadvantage is the unusually complicated and time-consuming federal income tax form that trusts must use.

Nonprofit corporations, cooperatives, and partnerships. Attorney Lee Goldstein, author of *Communes, Law*

& *Commonsense*, believes that "probably the preferred legal form for communes in most states is the nonprofit corporation." Commune members can do most of the legal work themselves, he says, so the lawyer's fees for setting up a nonprofit corporation is lower than the fee for a trust. Documents don't need to be revised when the membership changes, and the record owners can't sell the house without the others' knowledge. Goldstein also points out that a nonprofit corporation can attain tax-exempt status by showing that its purpose is charitable, educational, religious, or scientific. However, most communes would be hard-pressed to convince the Internal Revenue Service on this point. Another difficulty is that when a tax-exempt organization dissolves, the assets must be turned over to another tax-exempt organization. This means the members of a tax-exempt commune could never sell their house and recover their investment.

Goldstein's book explains two more forms of organization that, while used by few communes, are additional possibilities. These are the cooperative, which only some states recognize as a separate form of organization, and the partnership, which has a serious disadvantage — any individual partner can be held wholly liable for the partnership's debts.

Tax Implications of Communal Ownership

As already mentioned, commune members are entitled to income tax deductions based on the contribution each member makes to mortgage interest payments and local real estate taxes. The form of organization you choose probably won't affect the size of these deductions. However, a lawyer may have suggestions about ways to reduce members' tax liability in specific cases. Some groups toy with the idea of shifting the income tax deductions to the high-income members who have the greatest need of deductions. The idea is appealing but, according to the Internal Revenue Service, illegal.

Insurance for Groups

Like any family that owns a home, your group will need liability insurance. Some lawyers make much of the fact that personal injury suits cannot be brought against individual commune members if they have chosen a corporate form of ownership. If a visitor slips on your steps, the suit goes against the legal entity, not against any individual. However, if the corporate entity has neglected to obtain insurance, the individual owners can be named as defendants. One way or the other, the need for liability insurance is inescapable.

The cheapest way to obtain liability, fire, and theft insurance is to buy all of these coverages in a single package called a homeowner's policy. This policy is sold to a family that occupies its own house. Whether a commune can obtain homeowner's insurance depends on rules that vary from state to state and on the way these rules are interpreted, which varies from one insurance company to the next.

To some companies, a "family" exists only when household members are related by blood, marriage, or adoption or when an unmarried couple lives together. Other companies recognize families whose members are not related in these ways, especially if the group has only four or five members. If your group is larger and some members are related by blood, marriage, or adoption or are unmarried couples, a company may decide that you qualify for homeowner's insurance. But since the insurance rules don't explain whether such a group is entitled to homeowner's coverage, the only way to find out is to check with an insurance agent.

When you apply for insurance you may be tempted to help your case by leaving some names off the application. This could easily turn out to be a mistake. If your house burns down and the insurance company proves that you misrepresented yourselves, it can refuse to pay.

Here are three suggestions for a group that is going to buy a house and must have insurance:

1. Shop around. It is likely that some companies will offer to insure you at a lower rate than others. Try to get a homeowner's policy. You can always obtain another form of coverage—but it will cost more.

2. Find an insurance agent who is familiar with middle-class communes and sympathetic to this life-style. Since the insurance rules are vague and uncertain as they apply to communes, the right agent may be able to write a policy that another agent would not write. You may have to make a number of inquiries to find a sympathetic agent. Try asking other communes where they obtained their insurance. A local community information center (see Appendix A) might also be able to recommend an agent.

3. In many areas of the country, people who have difficulty obtaining insurance can get it through an industry pool called the Fair Access to Insurance Requirements Plan. One FAIR Plan official claimed that communal households should be able to obtain insurance at normal homeowner's rates through the plan. However, he hedged by adding that an inspection might be necessary and that the inspector mght discover an "unusual hazard" such as a heavy load on the electrical wiring caused by the energy requirements of a household of too many people. Such an "unusual hazard" would increase the cost of coverage.

Clearly, buying a house is not a simple project. It is a major undertaking. On the other hand, a group has more people to do the work. A task can be assigned to each member and the goal reached quickly. Once you own a house, you can relax in triumph—and be thankful that buying a house isn't a project that must be repeated every year.

APPENDIX C: THE COMMUNAL HOME OWNERSHIP AGREEMENT

When a group buys a house, it hopes to perpetuate feelings of closeness and warmth. Buying a house is a good way to do this—unless the good feelings are destroyed by a misunderstanding about ownership or finances. To make sure there will be no such misunderstandings, groups write a communal home ownership agreement. This agreement answers a number of important questions, such as who owns the house, how an ownership share may be transferred from one person to another, under what conditions the house may be sold, how the proceeds of a sale will be divided, what happens if an owner dies, and who pays for maintenance and repair.

DRAFTING AN AGREEMENT

Some communal ownership agreements are only one or two pages long. Your agreement doesn't have to be lengthy and you don't have to phrase it in legalese. (Some of the provisions quoted below, however, were written in legalese — by lawyers who live communally.) It is much cheaper to draft the agreement yourselves and then take it to a lawyer. If you live in an area where other communal households exist, you should be able to find a lawyer who is already familiar with this kind of agreement. This should also reduce your legal fees, since the lawyer will have less homework to do. The lawyer will read your draft, tell you whether it says what you want it to say, and perhaps change a few points to meet the requirements of law in your state. When you proceed in this fashion, your lawyer's services probably won't cost more than one hundred dollars or so, although it's a good idea to ask about the cost in advance.

Provisions

The sample provisions that appear below will help you draft your agreement. These provisions are numbered as in a legal contract and have been compiled from actual communal ownership agreements. The numbers are a convenient reference system for a group discussion of which provisions to include or modify. You may wish to copy some of them without change and modify others to meet your particular needs. And you may want to write some original provisions to deal with matters not covered here.

Heading. Choose a heading to put at the top of the first page. Titles that some groups have used are:

Agreement

General Agreement

Holding Agreement for Sunset House

Identification of parties and property. When more than three or four members are to become co-owners, the usual practice is for some members to buy property as "nominees" of the entire group. Names of the nominees appear on the loan application, the deed, and the communal ownership agreement. Names of the other members appear only on the communal ownership agreement. The provision can look like this:

1.1   Joe Schmitz, Marlene Leventhal, and Sally Forsyth hold the record title to the real prop-

erty at 1776 Blaine Avenue, Berkeley, Califor-
nia, as nominees for: Joe Schmitz, Marlene
Leventhal, Sally Forsyth, Earl Longworth,
Michael Young, and Ellen Hamilton.

If you have a small group and everyone's name appears
on all the documents, you can use this form:

1.2   The parties to this agreement are: Darlene
       Deveraux, Lloyd French, Judy Smith, and Eric
       Bloomgarten.

1.3   The property to which this agreement refers is:
       the real property at 1212 Pearl Street, Brooklyn,
       New York.

Legal description of property. If your agreement is to
be recorded, it should include the legal description of
your property as it appears on the deed.

Shares and tenancy. Communal ownership is "undivided." That is, John doesn't own the living room while
Sue owns the back yard and Frank owns the master
bedroom. Each owns a share of the entire house. The
amount each person has invested in the house can be
shown as a dollar figure or as a percentage or fraction of
the total downpayment. Most members of communal
groups hold their shares as "tenants-in-common." This
means that the share of a member who dies will pass to
the member's heirs. When property is held in "joint
tenancy with right of survivorship," the share of an
owner who dies will automatically go to the surviving
owners.

2.1   Frank Holly, Sue Harris, and Ellen Montague
       are owners of the property as tenants-
       in-common, with interests in the following
       proportions:
          Frank Holly $7,503.34 (60 percent)
          Sue Harris $3,500 (28 percent)
          Ellen Montague $1,500 (12 percent)

Another group chose this wording:

2.2   There are three undivided interests in the
       property, in the proportions set forth below,

held as a tenancy-in-common without right of survivorship.

> Abigail Wright owns a two-ninths interest. Bob Lefcourt owns a two-ninths interest. Lee and Arlene O'Neill own a five-ninths interest as joint tenants with right of survivorship.

Lee and Arlene are a married couple. If one dies, the other will automatically inherit the spouse's share of the house.

Survivorship. For some groups, choice of tenancy resolves the question of survivorship. Other groups create additional provisions specifying what happens upon a member's death.

3.3 Upon the death of a tenant-in-common, it is agreed that the remaining tenants-in-common shall purchase the interest of the deceased in the property. The purchase price shall be the book value of the deceased's interest determined on a cost basis. The purchase price shall be paid from insurance proceeds on the life of the deceased. Each tenant-in-common agrees to purchase insurance on his or her life in an amount not less than the said tenant-in-common's initial investment. The remaining tenants-in-common shall be named as the beneficiaries of the insurance. The proceeds of the insurance shall be used to purchase the interest of a deceased tenant-in-common and any excess proceeds shall be distributed to the estate of the deceased.

Another group agreed to this provision:

3.4 In the event of the death of any party to this agreement, the other parties shall have a first right of refusal to purchase the deceased's interest in the property at its fair market value. If no other party desires to exercise such a right, then other residents of the property shall have a second right of refusal, conditioned upon the prior approval of each party who holds an interest in the property. If no other party or resident desires to purchase the deceased's interest, it may be sold to any willing buyer, provided that such sale has the prior approval of each party who continues to hold an interest in the property.

"First right of refusal" means that the other owners get the first opportunity to buy the deceased owner's share. If they decide not to buy the share, then "other residents"—members of the commune who haven't invested in the house—get a chance to buy the share.

One group wrote a provision making it clear that a member's heir cannot become a member of the commune uninvited:

3.5 In the event that any party dies, his or her estate must sell his or her interest back to the other parties at the then book value of the interest being sold. Payment shall be made within ninety days....In no event shall the heirs, devisees, or legatees of a deceased party have any rights or obligations with respect to the ownership share of the deceased party except the right to receive payment for said share in accordance with the terms set forth above.

Loans. When one member buys an ownership share with money borrowed from another member, the group may want to clarify how the loan affects ownership of the house.

4.1 Any loans made by any party to any other party for the purpose of purchasing an interest in the property do not affect the ownership of the property as described above, except to the extent that a party's interest in the property may have been made security for such a loan.

Financial responsibility. It is necessary to identify the payments that members agree to make and specify what happens if someone fails to contribute financially to the group.

    5.1   Each party agrees to contribute an amount, monthly, to cover his or her pro rata share of the following costs: taxes, insurance premiums, upkeep, repair, maintenance, common furnishing, and principal and interest payments.

Another group agreed:

    5.2   Rents shall be established in amounts adequate to provide for the payment of all operating expenses (including payments of principal and interest on the two existing deeds of trust, taxes, insurance, maintenance, and repairs). Any extraordinary expense shall be borne by the parties in proportion to her or his interest in the property.

A third group:

    5.3   Owners will decide by unanimous agreement the fair rent of each bedroom. If an owner defaults in rent payments for two consecutive months, he or she shall vacate the house, and the amount of rent past due shall be deducted from his or her individual ownership share.

    5.4   All owners and residents agree to pay $7.50 a month to the maintenance fund.

Improvements. It is useful to distinguish between maintenance and improvements. Improvements are major projects that add to the value of the house — for example, putting in a new heating system, remodeling the kitchen, or adding a deck or a swimming pool. If the house is sold, the price will be higher because of the improvement. Groups keep a record of the amount each member invests in any improvements. When the house is sold, the amount an individual owner receives is proportional to the amount the owner invested in the downpayment and in improvements.

6.1   Maintenance or repair work is that work necessary to maintain the value of the house. Members agree to carry out all maintenance or repair work necessary to maintain the value of the house and to pay for it out of the maintenance fund.

6.2   Improvements are projects that add to the value of the house. Members will undertake such improvement projects as they unanimously agree to.

Sweat equity. This term refers to equity that members acquire through their labor on the house. When a group undertakes a major improvement—such as remodeling part of the house or building an addition—it is important to decide in advance whether anyone will be compensated and, if so, to what extent. One group bought a house with the expectation that everyone would pitch in to remodel the kitchen and several other rooms. Some members did work steadily on the house, but others gradually became involved in other projects. Four years later, when the possibility of eventually selling the house was raised, its value had increased many thousands of dollars thanks to the labor that some members had contributed. The group was in a quandary about how to divide the proceeds of a sale because there was no way even to estimate how much each member had worked.

The most common way of compensating members for their labor is to increase their ownership share in proportion to the number of hours they work.

7.1   An owner who works on an improvement will receive three dollars an hour. The amount earned will be applied to the worker's ownership share, or the worker may be compensated in some other manner by unanimous agreement. Workers will keep a record of the hours they work.

If you have members who cannot afford to invest in the

downpayment, you might consider making it possible for them to acquire a share of the house through sweat equity.

Transfer of shares. Groups need to provide a way for members to buy one another out and a way for members to sell shares to a new member who joins the group. Because commune members want to keep the right to choose their housemates, most agreements allow sale of a share to an outsider only when the buyer is acceptable to all residents of the house.

A share cannot be sold until its value is determined. This may be difficult since the only sure way to establish the market value of a house is to sell it. Some groups call for an appraisal when a share is to be sold. An alternative method of pricing shares is to have a formula that allows you to calculate the "book value" of the house. For example, book value could be the purchase price, plus the cost of improvements, plus 10 percent per year to cover appreciation. (People who believe that no one should profit from providing housing would omit appreciation from the formula. One effect of this omission is to hold down the price of a share and make it easier for others to buy in.)

8.1   If one tenant-in-common desires to sell or otherwise dispose of his or her interest, he or she shall offer it to other other tenants-in-common. They shall have ninety days to accept the seller's offer. The purchase price is payable in five equal annual installments, the first installment due upon acceptance of the offer. The remaining four installments shall bear interest at 7 percent. If the remaining partners do not exercise their right, the seller may sell or otherwise dispose of his or her interest to a third party, provided that if the third party will be living in the house, the remaining tenants shall have the right to approve or disapprove of the sale to the third party.

The provision above doesn't specify how the price of a share will be determined. The one below does:

8.2 In the event that any one of us wishes to leave the house and terminate his or her ownership interest in the same, the parties remaining in the house shall buy his or her interest at a price and on terms and conditions to be agreed upon by and between the leaving party and the remaining parties. In the event that no mutually acceptable price can be arranged, the house shall be assessed by two competent real estate appraisers — one selected by the party wishing to leave the house and the other selected by the parties wishing to remain — and the parties wishing to remain in the house shall purchase the interest of the party wishing to leave the house at a figure equal to the average net value of the leaving party's interest in the house (determined by multiplying that party's percentage interest in the house by a sum equal to the mean appraised value of the house less the value of any encumbrances then existing against the house). The respective ownership shares of the remaining parties shall thereafter be adjusted to reflect the contributions they have each made to the purchase of the leaving party's interest in the house. The leaving party shall therefore be paid the amount set upon his or her interest in the house in cash within a period of six months from the date the price is determined.

Another group took great care to ensure that no misunderstandings would complicate the sale of a share and departure of an owner:

8.3 Leaving parties must give remaining parties at least sixty days' written notice of their intention to move out and their intended termination date.

8.4 If leaving parties move out before sixty days after giving notice, the termination date is deemed to be sixty days after notice is given.

8.5 All rights and obligations of leaving parties remain in effect until the termination date.

8.6 On the termination date, the leaving parties shall convey their interests in the property to the remaining parties. In return, the remaining parties shall be obligated to pay the leaving parties for their interests in the property, according to the terms set forth below.

8.7 If within thirty days after the original termination date, some of the remaining parties decide to move out of the property and so notify all of the other parties in writing, then such parties shall be considered leaving parties, in the same position as the original leaving parties. The termination date shall be changed to a date not more than thirty days after such notification, and shall apply to all leaving parties. The provisions of this agreement shall apply to all leaving parties as if they had all decided to move out at the same time.

8.8 If within thirty days after the original termination date, the remaining parties decide to sell the property and so notify the leaving parties in writing, then the provisions above shall not apply. Instead, all of the parties shall sell the property together and divide the proceeds as if there had been no decision by some parties to move out.

Terms of payment to leaving parties by remaining parties:

8.9 The principal amount to be paid is the fair market value, as of the termination date, of the leaving parties' interests in the property, as determined by an independent appraiser, at leaving parties' expense.

8.10 If the termination date is within one year of the date we purchased the house, the value of the real property shall be deemed to be the original purchase price, plus other amounts spent to repair and improve the real property.

8.11 The first payment shall be made within sixty days after the termination date. The amount of the first payment shall be the lesser of: 20 percent of the principal, or one thousand dollars.

8.12 The remainder shall be paid in twenty-four approximately equal monthly installments, beginning ninety days after the termination date.

8.13 The rate of interest is 8 percent per year, compounded annually, computed on the outstanding balance, beginning on the termination date.

8.14 The remaining parties may make any payments sooner than scheduled, with a corresponding reduction in the interest accrued.

8.15 Security for payment of the amount owed shall be the remaining parties' interests in the property.

8.16 The remaining parties may sell any part of their interests in the property after the termination date. If they do so, any cash realized by such sale shall be immediately used to pay the debt then owed to the leaving parties. If, after this is done, the value of the equity interests in the property retained by the remaining parties is less than the amount then owed to the leaving parties, such excess shall be immediately paid to the leaving parties by the remaining parties.

A real estate appraiser receives a professional fee — one hundred dollars and up. But real estate agents may agree to estimate the value of a house for free. So one group provided that:

8.17 The fair market value shall be determined by

averaging separate appraisals made by three independent real estate brokers selected one by each party. However, if any dispute arises as to the value thus established, the disputing party may at her or his own expense obtain an appraisal from a licensed real estate appraiser, approved by each party, and such appraisal shall be conclusive.

Sale of the house. It is important to agree on the conditions under which the house may be sold and to specify how the proceeds will be distributed.

9.1   We may, of course, sell the house at any time by mutual consent of all parties. The net proceeds will be divided among us in accordance with our respective percentage interests in the house as set forth above, including investments in improvements and sweat equity.

One group expected that one or two members would leave town in a few years and want to recover their investment in the house. No one knew whether the remaining members would have enough money to buy out the departing members. The group decided to handle the problem like this:

9.2   An owner may sell his or her share to another owner at any time.

9.3   Within two years of the date of this agreement, the house may be sold only by unanimous agreement of all owners.

9.4   After two years from the date of this agreement, an owner who wishes to sell his or her share must first offer it to the other owners. If agreement to buy the share is not reached, the owner may demand sale of the house. Such a demand must be presented in writing to the other owners. A date when the house must be placed on the market will be set as follows:

(1) If the demand to sell is made by an owner of a 50 percent or greater inter-

est in the property, the house must be placed on the market within three months of the date of the demand to sell.

(2) If the demand to sell is made by an owner of an interest of between 20 and 50 percent, the house must be placed on the market within six months of the date of demand.

(3) If the demand to sell is made by the holder of a share of less than 20 percent, the house must be placed on the market within twelve months of the date of demand.

9.5   If during the above waiting periods other owners become financially able to buy out the owner who demands sale, the owner who demands sale will sell his or her share to them, under the terms specified elsewhere in this agreement.

9.6   If during the above waiting periods the other owners locate a buyer who wishes to buy the share, it will be sold to that buyer under the terms specified elsewhere in this agreement, provided the buyer is acceptable to all remaining owners.

Amendments.

10.1 Any provision of this agreement may be amended by unanimous vote of the owners. All proposed amendments must be presented in writing and signed by all owners to become effective.

Arbitration.   If an agreement is drafted with care, the chance of a dispute later on is small. However, some groups provide for arbitration in case a dispute does arise. Taking a suit to court is expensive and years may pass before the matter is finally settled. By comparison, arbitration is cheap and quick.

11.1 Any dispute or controversy arising under this agreement shall be settled by arbitration. In case of such dispute or controversy, a majority of the parties shall select an impartial arbitrator, and the decisions of such arbitrator shall be binding and conclusive to all parties and may be enforced by any party in a court of competent jurisdiction.

Date and signatures. Provide a space at the bottom of your agreement for the date and place of signing and the signature of each party.

APPENDIX D:
THE
SINGLE-OWNER
HOUSE

Sometimes a communal house is owned solely by one member or by a couple who are members. These single-owner households are created in several ways. A divorce or the death of a spouse often leaves an individual without a family but with a large house suitable for family living. This person can recruit others to live communally in the house. Other single-owner communes are begun by married couples who want more adults to interact with their children and share the burden of childrearing. As mentioned in Chapter Two, such a couple may invite other adults to share their home. Sometimes a single individual who wants to found a commune buys a house and invites others to move in. Finally, some single-owner communes are started by groups that include only one member or one couple with enough capital to invest in a house. This member or couple buys the house and everyone contributes to the monthly payments.

THE OWNER'S MOTIVES

Often the person who owns the house wants to be an equal member of a communal family and also happens to be a self-aware person who communicates well with others. With this owner, the chances of success in a single-owner household are at least as good as in any other kind of communal household. Some of the most harmonious and longest-lived communes are owned by an individual or a couple.

But some owners have expectations they are not fully aware of when they start a commune, which can cause problems. For example, one man bought a house and founded a commune without realizing that he would play the role of "father." He was at least ten years older than most of those who joined, and he made himself responsible for paying all the household bills and collecting the amount each member owed. The others soon rebelled against what they saw as his parental authority. The phone bill went three hundred dollars into arrears and one member fell two months behind in his rent. Matters improved when the owner realized what was happening and started to give up his paternal role. The telephone, which had been listed under his name, was relisted under a fictitious name, and the group began to rotate the responsibility for paying bills and collecting money from members. Another man who founded a commune came closer to playing the role of a child than a parent. He wanted the others to take care of him by, for example, washing the dishes that he used but "forgot" to clean up. This conflict was not resolved until members became angry enough to move out.

If you, or you and your spouse, plan to become the owners of a communal house, you might pause to consider what your motives are and to decide how realistic your expectations are. Similarly, someone who plans to join a single-owner household would do well to discover in advance what the owner expects.

THE GROUP'S EXPECTATIONS

This book has pointed out that those who live in middle-class communes believe strongly that all members of a communal group should be equal. People who want a father figure to tell them what to do don't live in middle-class communes; they choose a guru-led spiritual group. People who want a manager to run their household don't live in a middle-class household either; they choose a boarding house. So it's a safe bet that the members of a middle-class commune will all want an equal voice in day-to-day decisions, and will resent it if the owner (or any other member) tries to make unilateral decisions.

Single-owner households function best when, for the purposes of day-to-day living, the owner is an equal member of the group with no more authority than any other member. This means, for example, that what the owner wants has no more weight than what anyone else wants in regard to housekeeping standards, cooking, and shopping, how long guests may stay, and so on. These day-to-day decisions are made by consensus just as in any other commune. At the same time, the members recognize that the owner does have special authority in certain carefully defined areas. Usually the owner has final authority concerning house maintenance and repairs, and the owner is the only person who can decide whether to sell the house. With those exceptions, the owner is a member with no special prerogatives.

It helps to define the areas in which the owner will have special authority before anyone else moves into the house. When this is done, the rights of the owner and of the group can be balanced to everyone's satisfaction. Neither owner nor members will feel that the other has too much power. A good way to clarify everyone's expectations is to answer the questions that follow.

Who Chooses the Members?

In a boarding house, the owner or manager decides who may move in. But in a commune the group as a whole selects its members. It may be necessary for the owner to make a start by selecting the first member of a single-owner household. Thereafter, the normal selection process (described in Chapter Seven) is followed. The owner and first member agree on the third member; then the three of them pick the fourth member; and so on. This process gives everyone the right to veto any candidate.

In a single-owner house there is a danger the veto might be used unfairly. Some members could exercise one veto after another while they waited for the "perfect" candidate to come along. These vetoes wouldn't cost them anything if a room stood vacant, generating no rent: It would be up to the owner to make up the loss. Because this would be unfair to the owner, the members of single-owner communes agree that when rent is lost because a room has been vacant for more than one month, all members will contribute equally to make up the deficit. They also make an agreement to prevent deficits: Anyone who plans to move out must give at least a month's notice or, if notice isn't given, must pay the last month's rent. This agreement ensures that the remaining members will have enough time to interview candidates and find a good replacement member before any rent is lost.

To sum up, single-owner communes prevent conflict over the selection of new members by making three agreements that complement one another:

1. The group as a whole selects its members using the "veto system."

2. All members agree to contribute equally to make up for any rent lost because of an unfilled vacancy.

3. A member who plans to move out gives at least a month's notice or, failing that, pays the last month's rent.

Will Anyone Derive an Unfair Financial Advantage?

Occasionally a commune has a member who habitually falls behind in rent payments and moves out still owing rent. It is common practice to guard against this by requiring new members to pay their first and last month's rent in advance. A new member who is short on cash may be allowed to pay the last month's rent in installments after moving in. Asking for rent in advance may sound too cold and businesslike for a commune, but it is important to establish the expectation that members will be responsible about paying rent. Some people are encouraged to be irresponsible if they get the idea that the owner of the house—or the group as a whole—might provide free accommodations.

Sometimes there are bad feelings in a single-owner commune because the members believe the owner is collecting more than a fair amount in rent. An owner can avert this kind of conflict by making sure everyone understands the financial basis of the household. When this is done, it should be possible for everyone to feel that the financial arrangements are fair and work to the mutual advantage of the owner and the other members. It was the owner alone who invested a large sum of money in the downpayment, and it is the owner alone who bears the risk that the house might collapse during an earthquake or that the neighborhood might deteriorate and reduce the value of the house. In some communes the owner is in charge of maintenance and repairs and is responsible for all of the bookkeeping that is part of home ownership. In recognition of these contributions by the owner, the other members pay a share of the house payments, so that over the years the owner's equity in the house steadily increases. If the owner eventually decides to sell, this equity will be worth a lot of money.

In single-owner households, as in other communes, a rent is assigned to each room, including the owner's room. The total of these room rents is set high enough to cover all housing costs, including mortgage and interest payments, maintenance and repairs, insurance, and so forth. In some single-owner households, the total rent is set high enough to cover these costs and to yield a modest return on the owner's investment (in one commune, for example, the owner earns 6 percent a year on money invested in the downpayment). When the owner receives interest, the assumption is that since the owner is the only person with capital tied up in the house, the owner deserves an annual return on that investment. When the owner receives no interest, the assumption is that the owner will be amply compensated if the house is sold.

Especially during a period of high inflation when it may be necessary to increase rents often, it is important that the members understand to what use their rent money is put. One commune, owned by a couple, holds an annual budget meeting during which all housing costs are explained. When the members know how their money is spent, they can see that the owner is not exploiting them financially — unless, of course, they actually are being exploited. This does happen occasionally. In one household, room rents were high compared to the rent paid by members of other communes. The owner had purchased the house with a ten-year mortgage loan instead of the normal thirty- or forty-year loan and had passed his high interest payments on in full to the members. This points to the simplest and perhaps the best test of fairness: If the rent paid by members is moderate or low, the owner is not taking advantage of them.

Who Decides About Repairs and Improvements?

Since the owner is the only member who has invested in the downpayment, the owner is normally given the ultimate right to decide when the exterior will be painted and what color; whether a room will be added or remodeled; and so on. However, the members usually expect to be consulted fully before any repair or improvement project is undertaken. In the annual budget meeting mentioned above, the whole household discusses projects that the members or the couple who own the house would like to see carried out. Costs are estimated and taken into account later in the meeting when room rents are set for the following year. If members want a project badly enough, they agree to pay for it by raising rents a few dollars. If the project is one that the owners want but that generates little enthusiasm among the members, the couple may agree to pay for it. In one commune the group had trouble deciding who would pay for the addition of a bathroom. Eventually the members agreed to contribute their labor to build it, and the owners agreed to pay for the materials.

Who Decides on Domestic Arrangements?

No one is likely to question the owner's authority to arrange the furniture or decide how a common room will be used—in a boarding house. Similarly, a dormitory housemother might have unquestioned authority to direct cleaning operations. But in a commune, decisions about use of space and levels of cleanliness and order are made by the group as a whole. An owner's attempt to exercise some special influence in these matters won't be appreciated. For example, a widow who turned her house into a commune got a cool reception when she drew up a list showing where everything was to be put away in the kitchen. If an owner has expectations about how certain rooms are to be used, it would be a good idea to state these expectations clearly and to secure everyone's agreement in advance.

What Responsibility Will Members Have to the Owner's Children?

If the owner has kids and expects members to baby-sit or to become close friends with the children, it is important to spell this out in advance, and to reach agreement about what compensation—if any —the members should receive for their participation in childcare. The possibility of conflict involving the owner's children is noted in Chapter Two in the paragraph on central family communes, and the checklist in Chapter Seven contains questions that help to clarify expectations concerning children.

BIBLIOGRAPHY

Abrams, Philip, and McCulloch, Andrew. *Communes, Sociology, and Society*. Cambridge: Cambridge University Press, 1976.

Alam, Sterling. "Middle-Class Communes: A Contemporary Model." *International Journal of Modern Sociology* 6 (Spring 1976): 181-88.

Best, James S. *Another Way to Live: Experiencing Intentional Community*. Wallingford, Pa.: Pendle Hill Publications, 1978.

Bradford, David, and Bradford, Eva. "A Model for a Middle Class Commune." Offset. 1972.

Bradford, David, and Klevansky, Simon. "Four Types of Middle Class Communes." Offset. Stanford University Graduate School of Business, Research Paper No. 207. May 1974.

————. "Non-Utopian Communities —The Middle-Class Commune." Offset. Stanford University, no date.

Brown, L. Dave, and Brown, Jane C. "The Struggle for an Alternative: A Case Study of a Commune." *Human Organization* 32 (Fall 1973): 257-66.

Coakley, Michael, "A Family, Not Just a Roommate." *Chicago Tribune*, 7 September 1976.

"Communal Living Comes in from the Woods." *Money*, November 1976, pp. 87-88.

Constantine, Larry, and Constantine, Joan. *Group Marriage: A Study of Contemporary Multilateral Marriage*. New York: Collier Macmillan International, 1974.

Corr, Michael, and MacLeod, Dan. "Getting It Together." *Environment* 14 (November 1972): 3.

Danziger, Carl, and Greenwald, Mathew. *Alternatives: A Look at Unmarried Couples and Communes*. New York: Institute of Life Insurance, no date.

Dyer,Wayne. *Your Erroneous Zones*. New York: Funk & Wagnalls, 1976.

Eiduson, Bernice T. "Looking at Children in Emergent Family Styles." *Children Today*, July-August 1974, pp. 2-6.

Elm Lane Eight, The. "Commune in Disguise Flourishes in Suburbs." *New York Times*, 7 December 1975, p. R-1.

Fensterheim, Herbert, and Baer, Jean. *Don't Say Yes When You Want to Say No*. New York: Dell, 1975.

Ferrar, Jane. "The Experiences of Parents in Contemporary Communal Households." Offset. Urban Communes Project, Columbia University. 1976.

French, David and French, Elena. *Working Communally: Patterns and Possibilities*. New York: Russel Sage, 1975.

Gardner, Hugh. *Children of Prosperity: Thirteen Modern American Communes*. New York: St. Martin's Press, 1978.

Goldstein, Lee. *Communes, Law & Commonsense: A Legal Manual for Communities*. Boston: New Community Projects, 1974.

Gordon, Thomas. *P.E.T.: Parent Effectiveness Training*. New York: New American Library, 1970.

Greenwald, Jerry A. *Be the Person You Were Meant to Be*. New York: Dell, 1974.

"'Group Living' Catches On and Goes Middle Class." *U.S. News & World Report*, 25 February 1974, p. 38.

Hartman, Diane. "Still Mountain House: A Middle-Class Commune." *Denver Post* Contemporary Magazine, 7 November, 1976, p. 6.

Hershberger, Ann. "The Transciency of Urban Communes." In *Communes: Creating and Managing the Collective Life*, edited by Rosabeth Moss Kanter, pp. 485-91. New York: Harper & Row, 1973.

Hochstein, Rollie. "The Joys of a Shared Celebration in a New Kind of Family." *Woman's Day*, December 1975, p. 88.

Hollie, Pamela G. "More Families Share Houses with Others to Enhance 'Life Style.' Middle-Class Americans Join in the Trend." *The Wall Street Journal*, 7 August 1972, p. 1.

Holloway, Mark. *Heavens on Earth: Utopian Communities in America, 1680-1880*. 2nd ed. New York: Dover Publications, 1966.

Huxley, Aldous. *Island*. New York: Harper & Row, 1972.

Jaffe, Dennis. "A Family Commune." *Communities* 20 (May-June 1975): 4-7.

——. "Couples in Communes" Ph.D. dissertation. Yale University, 1975.

—— and Kanter, Rosabeth Moss, "Couple Strains in Communal Households: A Four-Factor Model of the Separation Process." *Journal of Social Issues* 32 (1976): 169-91.

James, Marlise. "A Commune for Old Folks." *Life*, 12 May 1972.

Johnston, Charley, and Deisher, Robert. "Contemporary Communal Childrearing: A First Analysis." *Pediatrics* 52 (September 1973): 319-26.

Kanter, Rosabeth Moss. *Commitment and Community: Communes and Utopias in Sociological Perspective*. Cambridge: Harvard University Press, 1972.

——, ed. *Communes: Creating and Managing the Collective Life*. New York: Harper & Row, 1973.

——. "'Getting It All Together': Some Group Issues in Communes." In *Doing Unto Others*, edited by Zick Rubin, pp. 27-37. Englewood Cliffs, N.J.: Prentice-Hall, 1974. (Abridged from the *American Journal of Orthopsychiatry* 42 [1972]: 623-42.)

—— and Halter, Marilyn. "The De-Housewifing of

Women: Equality Between the Sexes in Urban Communes." Paper presented at the Meeting of the American Psychological Association, Montreal, August 1973.

————; Jaffe, Dennis; and Weisberg, D. Kelly. "Coupling, Parenting, and the Presence of Others: Intimate Relationships in Communal Households." *The Family Coordinator*, October 1975, pp. 433-52.

Kelly, Dorothy. "House Sharing 'Families.'" *San Francisco Magazine*, August 1976, p. 26.

Mainardi, Pat. "The Politics of Housework." In *Sisterhood Is Powerful*, edited by Robin Morgan, pp. 447-54. New York: Random House, 1970.

Micossi, Anita. "Executing Ideals: A Reappraisal of Urban Communal Living." Ph.D. dissertation. University of California, Berkeley, 1976.

Mowery, Jeni. "Systemic Requisites of Communal Groups." *Alternative Lifestyles: Changing Patterns in Marriage, Family & Intimacy* 1 (May 1978): 235-61.

Oakley, Ann. *The Sociology of Housework*. New York: Pantheon Books, 1975.

Ogilvy, Jay and Heather. "Communes and the Reconstruction of Reality." In *The Family, Communes, and Utopian Societies*, edited by Sallie TeSelle. New York: Harper & Row, 1972.

Oster, Jerry. "Five Families Share Farm and Lives." *Miami Herald*, 16 February 1972.

Pascoe, Elizabeth Jean. "New Alternatives to Old-Age Homes." *McCall's*, July 1976, p. 49.

Schutz, William. *The Interpersonal Underworld* (a reprint edition of *FIRO*). Palo Alto, Calif.: Science & Behavior Books, 1966.

Sheehy, Gail. *Passages: Predictable Crises of Adult Life*. New York: E. P. Dutton, 1976.

Slater, Philip. *The Pursuit of Loneliness*. Boston: Beacon Press, 1970.

"Small Group Living Arrangements for the Elderly." *The Gerontologist* 18 (April 1978): 142-43.

Smith, Manual J. *When I Say No, I Feel Guilty*. New York: Bantam Books, 1975.

Smith, William O. "New Community I." *Communities* 20 (May-June 1975): 8-10.

Stanwood, Les. "Double Families." *Mothers' Manual*, July-August 1978, p. 39.

Steiner, Claude. "Cooperative Living." *Communities* 20 (May-June 1975): 14-16.

Stephen, Beverly. "A Middle-Class Commune in the Mission." *San Francisco Chronicle*, 27 October 1975, p. 17.

Stix, Harriet. "A Commune Connection: Consider Yourself at Home." *Los Angeles Times*, 9 May 1976, p. 1.

Tiger, Lionel, and Shepher, Joseph. *Women in the Kibbutz*. New York: Harcourt Brace Jovanovich, 1975.

Toffler, Alvin. *Future Shock*. New York: Random House, 1970.

Wax, Judith. "'It's Like Your Own Home Here.'" *The New York Times Magazine*, 21 November 1976, p. 38.

Webber, Everett. *Escape to Utopia: The Communal Movement in America*. New York: Hastings House, 1959.

Williamson, George. "A Second Look at the 'Family.'" *San Francisco Chronicle*, 19 January 1978.

Wolk, Susan Stanley. "How Three Families Live Together." *Redbook*, April 1976, p. 84.

Young, Marjorie and James. "Can Group Family Life Work?" *Parents*, August 1975, p. 42.

Zablocki, Benjamin D. *Alienation and Charisma*. New York: The Free Press, 1979.

Index